The Road to El Palmar

A Traveller on the West Coast of Spain

by

Mark DK Berry

Copyright

The Road to El Palmar by Mark DK Berry
Copyright © 2004 Mark DK Berry
First Edition: January 2019

All rights reserved. Without limiting the rights under copyright reserved above, no part of this publication may be reproduced, stored in or introduced into a database and retrieval system or transmitted in any form or any means (electronic, mechanical, photocopying, recording or otherwise) without the prior written permission of both the owner of copyright and the publishers.

Email requests to: mdkberry@outlook.com

Paperback: ISBN: 978-0-6485395-4-4
Ebook: ISBN: 978-0-6485395-3-7

All drawings within this book are the copyright of Mark DK Berry, exceptions are listed below with links to their respective free-from-copyright information.

1. Map of route:
https://commons.wikimedia.org/wiki/File:1799_Clement_Cruttwell_Map_of_Spain_and_Portugal_-_Geographicus_-_Spain-cruttwell-1799.jpg

2. Map of The Battle of Trafalgar:
https://commons.wikimedia.org/wiki/File:TrafalgarBattle.jpg

3. Line art drawing of a galleon. By Pearson Scott Foresman.
https://commons.wikimedia.org/wiki/File:Galleon_(PSF).png

Contents

Pleasure you can't measure..5
Wrong stop..11
A lesson in going with the flow..14
One-trick pony..19
Learning to busk...22
The fine art of writing..24
The white walls of Conil...30
Lesson two: efficiency..32
What's freedom anyway?..42
Meditation classes for the rich...48
El Palmar...52
This is the end...60
The way of the guitar...63
The Battle of Trafalgar..71
More pre-dawn musing...79
The sea...82
The wind..89
On the road again..98
Nights in white satin, never reaching the end...102
Is this really who I am now?..114
A change of perception..128
The history of atoms...136
City of wild Spanish horses...139
The pilgrim's end..150

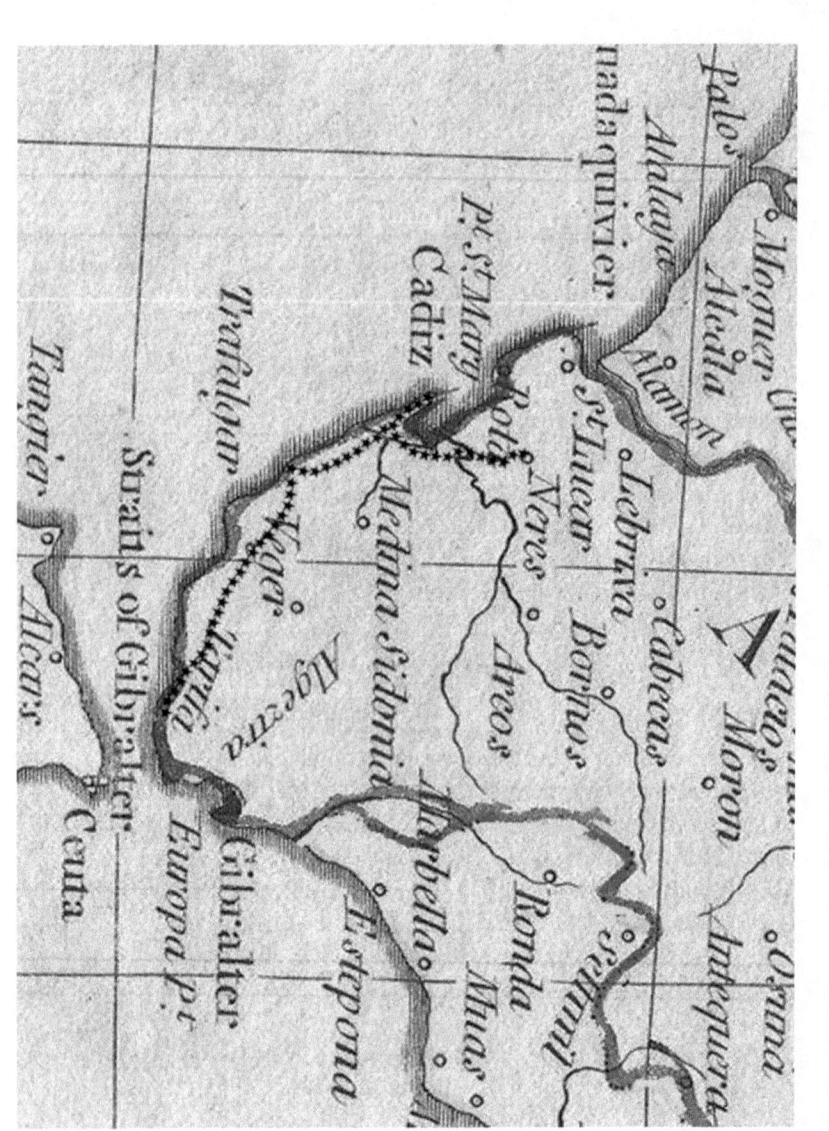

Map of Route

Pleasure you can't measure

It's good to get away from England this time, good to leave my worries and cares behind me, falling away like baggage from the plane as it launches off the runway, gravity pulling my emotions down into my gut with that familiar feeling of expectant pleasure mixed with a fear of the unknown. It's a clear day, mid-May 2004, as I watch the patchwork fields of England slip away below me. Matchbox cars, silicon-chip-like cities, scourged-out quarries, and muddy brown lakes. I am bound for Jerez in Spain. The seat beside me empty where she should have been and would have been if it weren't for a duty-bound hen night. Myself? Skipping on the related stag-do, the guilt far outweighed by a desperate need to get away for a while. I need to get out of the pressure cooker that my life has become, escape the city, my friends, my work, my obligations such as they are, and just leap into the unknown again.

I should have done my World Tours by now, sold platinum albums and retired to LA or South America to take up ranching with maybe a little whoring on the side, but things rarely work out the way we plan, huh? Still, at 37 it is nice to have the chance to do something new, nice to have been able to retain enough freedom that I can just book a flight and go. So this will be my first European Tour, seven days in Spain, my venue the streets. Where travellers and vagabonds play for coins and smiles and wannabe troubadours romanticise strangers with their dreams, a place where middle-class ne'er-do-wells enslaved to the rat-race, can run away to live out their fast-fading fantasies of being a *RocknRolla*.

I never made the south-west coast of Spain last time I was here, only got as far as Marbella. Maybe next time it will be southern Portugal and the Algarve, I have never been there. This time it is the Atlantic and the area between Cadiz and Tarifa that draws me. It is a destination that I have wanted to reach for some time, though I am not sure quite why I decided on it now. Maybe spiritual things await me

The Road to El Palmar

there, maybe memories of past-lives, or maybe my death. Whatever it is that awaits me, this feels like my first taste of freedom in a very long time.

How good this feels to be out on my own and getting away from my life. No guilt now, no pensive subtle pressure or feeling of urgency, no quiet and unexplained anxiety, no-one to answer to, or have to talk to, no fear, no tension, just me. Me, and the relaxed natural pace of the moment unfolding however it chooses to do so. A child-like feeling, a belief that adventure lies ahead, like how school summer holidays used to feel back when we believed in things. Yes, hints of summer and chains released, the world looks new and exciting, full of possibility. God, I so needed this, I didn't realise just how much until it hit me here now. I have been walking around like a goddamn zombie for so long. The last two years lie behind me like a trail of mysterious delirium, full to the brim with a complete lack of purpose. I feel like a man who has been lost for too long in the desert, chasing mirages he knows are not real and chasing them regardless because the alternative does not bear thinking about.

I never wanted to travel until recently, even though travel has marked my entire life, but in terms of travel by choice, Nicaragua was the first adventure I took on my own deliberately. I was convinced I was going to my death that time too, yet I returned surprisingly unscathed and bubbly, and with more dreams, direction, and inspiration than I had expected to have from such a short trip. Short like this one. Five days on that occasion, seven days for this trip. Nicaragua was certainly wild, and I realised *that* was what gave it it's magic. That magic is the very thing that seems to be missing from our safe and civilised worlds, or at least mine back in London. The Spirit hums out there in the wild, it's in the air, creating moments around you and in you too. Moments of magic. They seem so normal while you are in them that you barely realise their potency, nor do you acknowledge that you are closer to the jaws of Nature than you have ever been before, and nor do you want to be. Denial can be such a beautiful thing though. Yet, there is something very natural and invigorating in experiencing Nature nipping at your heels. The wild invigorates. Which makes me wonder why we strip it from our cities, rid it from our

Pleasure you can't measure

country-sides and gardens, our homes and offices in a deliberate exercise to manicure our souls and make life safe and controlled. I guess, unconsciously, we strive for immortality. Plastic and concrete certainly give us something close to that approximation, while experiencing Nature, the Spirit, or life's magic quality only ever reminds us that we are temporary.

I think the day that I take up smoking a pipe is nearly upon me. I find myself now with my pen between teeth, the other end is lodged into the little finger of my fisted hand, my thumb is lifting and dropping like a chimney flue as I puff air, and doing so I slip into a daydream. Feels very natural. What is it about a pipe that aids thinking, creates a calm in the spirit? It is strange to notice how some part of me is already familiar with it, yet it is something that I have never done. As if it is there already, just waiting to be discovered. How can that be? Some of my other habits seemed pre-designed in that same way. I guess having an innate ability for pipe-smoking must surely have its place and purpose in the world. Maybe it is for the thinking man, for to help him think.

The men in the seat behind me talk loudly of Arsenal and football, and I am suddenly reminded that I am a bit of a brain-twisted dandy. Football certainly bores me rigid. We don't have much choice in the way we are made, though we do have the option to take ourselves too seriously or just accept our quirks and get on with things. My task this year has been to find a way to switch off the tap of insanity that unleashes splurgum into my mind. I am not crazy yet, but something toxic in there is leaking, and I have ignored it for far too long. I figure it can still be fixed, but it is going to take time and effort. When you are drowning in chaos and mad thoughts that seem to bubble up from the depths of the mind, it is hard to work against that flow and harder still to switch it off. It's May, and I have been trying daily since the end of December to do just that. Five months, and I am beginning to find some success in my methods, but is it enough? Of all the things I have ever done, and all the places I have ever been, the one place that I would like to return to above all others is internal silence. The place where no thoughts are a-thinking. The complete opposite of what those fool teachers taught us in school. Educating us on how to be

The Road to El Palmar

thinking machines, wound-up tight, and with no clue how to undo that mind-driven tension. Shame on them for that. I came undone, though I guess I forced it in the worst possible way through a cocktail of recreational drugs. Even so, I got a glimpse of that inner stillness and it felt good. Now I am trying to stop all that druggie business and instead learn meditation to achieve it. Meditation, not medication. I figure if I want to stay sane in the 21st Century, I am going to need to learn it.

Islands pass below us. 150 trusting passengers in the hands of just two men. Are there no women pilots? I wonder why. Then I wonder for a minute what it might feel like should the plane explode. Metal tearing up in the pressure of icy-cold temperatures and high speeds. Bodies ripping apart in the sky so that bits of soft, squishy, flesh rain down on those below, along with about 1500 pints of blood. The thought used to scare me whenever I got on a plane but now, for some reason, I don't seem to care. It's not that the reality of it isn't tangible, far from it. Maybe it is because for the first time in a very long time I have the sensation that I am in the right place at the right time, doing the right thing, or maybe I have just become de-sensitised to the truth of it.

Pleasure you can't measure - it's written on the head-rest cover in front of me and on every seat in the plane. The seat ahead also contains an irritating girl who can't decide what angle her chair-back should be at. I get the urge to poke my foot in the gap between the seat and the chair-back. She'd jump like a cat if I could tickle her butt with the tip of my toes. I feel like being bad, and that feels good.

This is a great day! Finally, after more than two years, I get one again. Life is too generous surely, sire. I don't even have the urge to get obliteratingly drunk. I almost feel like talking to people that I don't know. Maybe ask my neighbour what their thoughts are on what it would feel like if the plane exploded. Maybe that is pushing it a bit. I know this good feeling won't last, it never does. It is just the holiday highs. The honeymoon period caused by the illusion of freedom. It is the moment of ecstasy that we all spend the rest of the year working towards. For a moment, it is like having sex with life itself. I want to fuck life right here and now in the gangway of this plane for being so damned beautiful. *Pleasure you can't measure*, sure, but how come most of

Pleasure you can't measure

the rest of the time it's just a pain I can't explain?

Strange textures in the white fields below making the shapes of horses. The Spirit of the earth looking back at me. Hang on, suddenly everything down there is shaped like horses. What's going on? When my eyes look, my mind makes out the shape and structures of the world. The rational part of us loves that. Everything has it's place and separation, borders and order. But then the other part of my mind sees completely different images and patterns in those same things. It has shape but is fluid and changes, it flows like a current. Too much LSD? You may be right. The horse shapes are gone now, but I just saw a penguin, and now it is back to normal except for the spider's webs of the cities. It is kind of pretty from up here. The overall colour now more sandy than green. Some dark, black, woods there and forests too. Everything so square and uniform. Everything so organised. Somehow it blocks out the natural. We are in the age of immortal plastic, and I am probably the last of a dying kind of creature because I care that we don't give in to that Blade Runner-esque world. Maybe it is inevitable. I feel old, curious, and a bit lost in modernity. I don't fit in, but I can't run away either. The war is over, for now, we live in peace-time. Of course, war still rages in far distant countries but here in Plastic-land, death is of a different kind. It's a death created by cutting off the senses from the inside. Cutting off the link to the Spirit of life. Cutting us off from the source by dulling the environment, making it 'safe'. Then letting the soul of a person buzz and stew in its own short-circuit, a fusing of bio-electrical static until it reaches maximum ionisation and then just implodes, generally making a big bloody mess. Everything is in a state of chaos really, which is probably why we so desperately seek order. And now...I need to take a piss.

That's better. The ground below is starting to take on more natural, random shapes again. This is promising, maybe Spain holds some of the wildness that I felt in Nicaragua. It seemed perfect out there at first, yet I knew death might come to visit a little too easily. I went there looking for a place to live, somewhere, maybe in the middle of that magic. It did not have to be Nicaragua necessarily, but I wanted to find a place to plant a flag and build, if not a new world, something. Maybe build a bridge back to the Spirit, if it could be done. The bridge between our ancestral spirits and the immortal, plasticised and civilised world that people, like myself, live but feel dead in. I quickly realised that Nicaragua was too far away, too corrupt, and too deadly. Spain is now my next choice to visit to see it's potential. Australia might have been my third, but they won't let me move there at my age.

Giant lakes down there now, a healthy dark blue. Though it is mostly dry, barren land, with desert-like quality, it must be Spain. Ah-ha…announcements - 80 miles North of Seville and 125 miles to touchdown. A slight nervousness kicking in. Check my watch, it's 10:30 am. Barely a word of Spanish to my vocabulary, my adventure is about to begin, a craving for cigarettes burning lightly within me, but I am happy. And it is worth remembering that, and squeezing something from the moment, to drink it, to savour it, and to enjoy it. *Pleasure you can't measure.* Rarer than a shooting star and just as fleeting and unpredictable. For some reason, that I cannot fathom, it is how my life feels right now. Here we go, get ready to let it all begin, landing is imminent. May it be death or glory, just please no more bland routines, and for god's sake get me away from this discussion about Arsenal.

Wrong stop

I land at roughly 10:30 am English time, 11:30 am in Spanish. By midday I make Jerez train station, having paid 11 euros to get there in a whistling taxi. The driver seems upset that I don't have change, or that I don't tip, or maybe he just doesn't like me, I am not sure.

"No speaky Espagbol, mate." I tell him by way of explanation, as I alight from his car.

I am still on London time and feel the need to rush and panic about everything. The train ticket to Cadiz costs two and a half euros. Seems cheap. Will take an hour. Where from? There is a question.

All the land seemed flat as I landed, somewhat uninteresting. Initial ecstasy already giving way to an urge for whisky and a numbing of the senses. I resist and instead begin to try to decipher the timetables. I ask people questions in pigeon-Spanish and eventually I find the train - I think - all thanks to a lady from Netherlands helping me out. Young boy asks me for money, but I laugh at him. I can always count on being approached by the beggars and drug dealers of any language. Train still in station at 12:15 pm. Maybe there was no need to launch myself and my belongings in quite such the desperate rush that I did. I guess London pace will wear off me soon enough. I am feeling hungry. At least I have a seat and it seems pretty empty in the carriage. No sooner do I think this than kids invade the train. Christ, there must be a hundred of them. So much for a quiet, serene journey. Kids always have foghorn voice boxes.

I didn't fancy staying in Jerez. Felt too much like a city, and I needed to get out. Nice statues on roundabouts and I think that I missed the city centre, but the place seemed easy going as I drove past some of it in the taxi, nothing of great interest or beauty from what little I could see. Lots of pictures of horses, and adverts about horse shows. Horses for courses. I saw a poster advertising Ministry of Sound and Plump DJ's tour dates. English aural invasion.

A temperature meter on the train says it is 25 degrees. Eventually

The Road to El Palmar

the doors close and the train begins to move off. We are fast out the city and cutting through small, frequent hills, then past industrial works. I can see mountains to the south. A pretty blond girl watches me write from a few seats away. A fat boy lounges like a beached seal on the seats just in front of me. Outside the window there are donkeys lost in long grass and old houses in rubble, good only for nesting birds. The animated, in-train foghorns shout and whistle and screech and then decide to sing a bit. Little darlings. We follow roads and power pylons, and sometimes a wide muddy river. I wonder how this adventure could possibly get more interesting. Then as if in answer, we are onto the endless expanse of flat land with nothing in it at all. An old man, with a face like a monkey, tries to chat up the lady from Netherlands.

The stop at Puerto de St Maria seems quaint. It is my first sign of the sea. Wide salt-flats and a big industrial estuary. The pretty girl still watching me looks away whenever I look up. The tease. Every place, every culture, has its own inherited way of dealing with people. I get the feeling the Andalusians are quietly interested in what you are, and what you are doing, but so far they seem quick to feign disinterest as soon as you react to their observations. Kids in England would be taking the piss out of my writing by now and probably picking a fight. These little monkeys don't seem too bothered, and actually aren't at all rude, just a bit noisy. But not being rude is something, it's a nice change. It makes me think about how aggressive London has become, or maybe it was always that way, or maybe it is just me. I wonder if I am tired of London finally, it has been 15 years since I arrived there from Oxford.

More vast expanse, and what seems like thick grass in flat swamp land. God, I hope the surf is good or else this holiday could be done for, I had come with a hope of getting in the waves. No wonder no one comes out here. I can understand why Laurie Lee only lasted a day in this region before travelling South to Gibraltar. But then maybe this seemingly dead zone will be ideal for me. No tourists so far, I guess these grassy flats hold little for us. A good looking woman joins the train. She keeps staring too, this time I'm almost intimidated. Oh man, the kids are singing again and clapping now.

Wrong stop

Bahia Sur looks even nicer than the last place. Orange white buildings. The kids get off, finally. I don't see a beach or sea here, but maybe it is there, especially given the name. Then we are out again, into even flatter country, how is that possible? I am starving now and only halfway to Cadiz, and then I spot the sea again. Right by it, I was, and there is no surf at all. The wind is strong out there all the same, and the sun burns down. No waves whatsoever, the Atlantic has done me again. It is like the Mediterranean here, nothing but gentle lapping waves. How can that be? I don't understand waves yet. I thought the Atlantic was a bloody great big ocean, so what the hell are those ripples? Without any warning, the next stop is Cadiz Cortadura. What? Cadiz or Cadiz Cortadura? Maybe there is more than one station. Sudden panic. I bail out of the train, just in case.

Typical. I have jumped out four stations too soon. It must mean Cortadura in the *land* of Cadiz. Hang on...

A train rolls in almost straight away, but however hard I push the buttons the doors don't open. I push them pretty hard. The train rolls off leaving me feeling stupid. Now what? I see a guy in the window, he looks bemused, a lone traveller with a rucksack and guitar, and his hair messy and in need of a cut, like a white Shaft, but not.

At 1:05 pm I sit in the heat and try to work out how to open train doors. According to my timetable... the next one is an hour away at least. I can't leave the station without cashing in my ticket, and I don't see anywhere here to go. There are no people at this station nor anything much outside of it, from what I can tell. It's all roads and emptiness. All I can do is wait and ponder on my dismay at the state of the surf in this place. I can see it over there. Maybe it will be better at Cadiz, if I ever get there. I am glad that I got the early flight, but my thirst for whisky just went up a notch.

A lesson in going with the flow

I don't have a great time at Cortadura train station. The wind blows hard, and the traffic rattles by, as I wait the hour for my next train. I sink briefly into a spell of reflective melancholy. I consider some of the reasons I have taken this break away alone, and that increases my sense of despair and loneliness. Things are not great back home on a number of levels and it makes me feel sad until I find my way back to an emotional equilibrium. During my sashay into temporary platform depression for some reason a couple of memories came up along with it. Two events where people said things that I really did not wish to hear, and subsequently left me confused as to their intentions.

I met a girl in a club, many years ago. I say 'met' but really I mostly pounced on her, which is probably a more accurate way of putting it, though she didn't seem to mind at the time, and I guess it worked because she invited me home quite soon after. Before letting me sleep with her, she insisted on reading my Tarot cards. I was familiar the cards, having dabbled, but what she said left me speechless.

"You will live a worse and worse life and die a terrible death."

Those were the exact words, because you tend to remember such things. I never did understand quite what motivated her to say it, though I wondered if it was something to do with the dynamic between us, maybe her way of getting me back for my pouncing abilities and what we both knew was coming later. I certainly never felt stupid enough to believe what she said. It did not bother me, so much as beckon the question - *is it possible to say anything worse to a person?* Those South Americans can be quite strange birds, she was Peruvian. I wondered, when she said it, if she was mad, but she seemed a full bag of shopping other than that.

The other memory, was from a supposedly good friend of mine at the time, though he turned out to be a somewhat dubious gentleman. He once made a prediction about three people who were in the room

A lesson in going with the flow

with him. It came out of the blue, this announcement that he had a prediction for us. He then shared everyone's out loud, but refused to tell me mine. Of course this made me try to coax it out of him. He did have an ability to be incredibly perceptive, but when he finally conceded to my demands, he told me that I was a suicide case. It smashed me to hear it. I had been going through a tough year as it was. I really despised him for that comment, it was totally unnecessary. Why would someone even say such a thing? Other than psychic manipulation, which is something he was definitely interested in, there was no real excuse for it. If someone is a suicide case, you certainly don't tell them like that. I did not buy into it, but it cut me up all the same, mostly because I could not fault his predictions with the other two. That freaked me out a little, but I figured he had planned it that way. I am still here and that was many years ago now. Our friendship deteriorated after that, so maybe that was a part of it. I no longer trusted him for a few other reasons that I won't go into here.

I do not know why I recalled those two things while stranded, somewhat angrily, at Cortadura station. The train finally arrived and my detour through monotony, Peruvian Tarot-card reading, and manipulative friendships along with that damn relentless wind, was over. Moving again, on to Cadiz, and things are back looking as they should. I am not sure why I relate this to you now, but it is in my journal, and that's what happened while I waited for a train at Cortadura station.

I leave the correct train station and look for a taxi. None come. I feel no surprise and decide to walk. Of course minutes later one passes me. I walk through what seems to be the old town. Thin streets, with tall, old looking sand-stone buildings. I find a plaza and what must be Cadiz's Cathedral. It's a port town with beaches to the west. Good beaches, hot, blustering, and blistering beaches, with fine golden sands and barely a soul on them, but definitely no surf. Disappointment, but only mild. I am more concerned to find my bed for the evening. I have a hostel name and address recommended by a quick search of the Internet before leaving - *Quo Qadis*.

I wait by the cathedral for a taxi. There's a cafe opposite with two

The Road to El Palmar

wandering buskers. An accordion player and his Tonto, a tambourine player. The tune is simple and a one-fingered affair. The tambourine man uses his tool to beg money from those seated in the cafe. Maybe this should be my evening's destination. It seems central, though I expect many buskers will appear at evensong. I should mention here, that this is to be my busking debut. I tried it once, pathetically, at The South Bank promenade in London last summer, and since that dismal day I have dreamed of heading to Spain armed only with my acoustic guitar and my wanderlust. Now, is that time, when dreams cross over to become reality, and we enter a new realm of experience for fear that we may miss the opportunity and then be forced to live in some kind of regret. I find it shocking to think that I have lived as a musician for this long, and yet never busked.

A taxi comes by. I hop in and head for the hostel. Three and a half euros and all the back-alleys the cheeky chap could find, but it's the price you pay for not knowing the lingo, and being a tourist. It's not far, and turns out that I could have walked it for free, but you have to pay for knowledge in this world.

I enter in and immediately become aware that I have entered backpacker heaven. This is the land of the white dread-lock student. The film 'The Beach' says it all. I guess I travel their world whether I like it or not, so I best like it. But these are not my people. The owner greets me dismissively and refuses to speak English, of course. Handing me over to yet another pretty young lady who is friendly and kind of sexy. I pay her sex, sorry six euros, and give her my passport number. Then, foolishly or otherwise because I have no choice, I leave my belongings in a back room. My belongings consist of one rucksack and an acoustic guitar. It is an advisedly safe place, and after being shown photos of the roof-terrace where I will be sleeping, I leave to investigate the beaches and check out the surf scene, if there is one. I wanted to camp, to tent. A tent is stuffed into my rucksack. My 40 euro per day budget is already stretching at the seams, but the owner, in his brief moment of willing communication, tells me there are no camp sites anywhere near there. I mention El Palmar, a place I heard of somewhere in my search. He looks at me askew, then I am shown a map and told it is 70km to the South, and near Conil. I ponder. I came out here to camp,

A lesson in going with the flow

and I mean that in the heterosexual sense, but 70km is too far for tonight, and so I book the roof-terrace, mainly because the photo makes me laugh, it looks like the aftermath of some rooftop party. I mention this.

"No party!" he exclaims, "Silence eleven!"

"Of course." I insist, trying to look angelic, but I read the reviews before I came.

Probably because I mentioned the word *party*, I am given a set of house-rules. I then leave, taking only my book and essentials that I really don't want to lose. It's 4 pm now, and I find a bus to take me where he says the surf may be. I walk Playa de la Victoria, and one mile later spot the singular surf shop, it is closed. Walking a few yards further on, I reach the end of Cadiz and find myself in…Cortadura. Sure enough, right by the train station where hours ago I clearly could have got out and walked. I am still stuck in London mode.

The wind suddenly whips up, and I feel a dark sensation just like I did at the station earlier. It starts to roar down the alley I am in. I fight against the wind and can barely walk. What the hell is this madness?

"Turn back!" it seems to shout, but I wont have it.

I move against it, on past the militia headquarters and round onto the noisy road that pissed me off so much earlier. I am convinced that on the other side I will find the surf, and at least 100 dudes whooping it up, and more importantly, escape this goddamn wind. I find only Cortadura beach and a dead bird. The wind was right, I should have listened. I turn around and am blown back to the main beach.

There I stop to drink, and write, and of course chain-smoke because that is what holidays are for. Stopping at Bar Bodega I quaff three cerveza, which I say a lot now… *three thervesa, three thervesa,* and then I write frantically. It feels good. I have bed and board sorted and am happy about that. The sun is high, too high for my white skin without the P20 suntan lotion I forgot to bring along. Maybe I can buy some. The sea is just over there. Things are going okay really. The suns a bit much, so I get in a shaded part of the outside bar instead, and then replace my need for food with ice cool lagers until my fingers ache with expression through the pen. Such a lost art in this day of computers and immortal plastic.

The Road to El Palmar

I consider Cortadura and the lesson it just gave me. A lesson in *going with the flow*. On the one hand I should have just got out the station when I messed up with the trains, then again, I would not have done the circuit of Cadiz if I had. Life holds something for us whatever direction we take, I guess. What I missed going this way the first time, who can say. But right now I am sat in a beach bar with a smiling waiter obeying my every wrist-flick, and once again I am incredibly happy and barefoot. Dousing the fire of the soul with beer, cold as the arctic, while being dazzled by sunshine, sand, and a sea so empty, that I wonder if this town isn't ripe for a touristic invasion. I didn't like Cadiz until I sat down here at this bar. I don't really know what I make of it now, but I feel a sense of pressure-less freedom, and I like that. I like it's emptiness, maybe it is just out of season. No surfers though, that surprises me, and kind of excites me too. The Atlantic, for all it's flat spells, holds the spirit of surf and for there to be no one out there at all on this mile long stretch of perfectly good beach, that tells me there is yet hope for the recently converted salty sea dog.

My watch strikes 5 pm and the sun still burns high. Pretty ladies abound in this town. None models, but they have a certain something worth enjoying. Not much English spoken though. Probably a good thing. I can picture the horror that this place would be if it was packed with sardine-like football hooligans, money pouring into it from British coffers. *Oi Oi, Savaloy!* and all that horror. Cadiz is a secret gem that could rise and sparkle in this age of tourism, if that age remains. Laurie Lee wrote in the nineteen-thirties at a time of civil unrest. I write in the Naughties in a time of consumption, opulence, obesity, and football hooliganism. Who knows what our future holds. Cut off from the main by barren flats as it is, maybe this is a small part of Spain that could avoid tourism to some extent. I am tempted to drink more, but something beckons me to the sea, to briefly tan and quicken to burn. Tomorrow I will leave here and head for Conil to find surf and to find camping, because I came here to camp, and I mean that in the heterosexual sense.

One-trick pony

It certainly looks as if Cadiz is a one-trick pony where the busking is concerned. After burning myself in the sun and getting pebble dashed on the beach by the wind, I find myself taking refuge from the heat and wind in a shaded corner of bar Morilla. It is 6:45 pm, and still like a microwave out there. I had to bow out before I sacrificed myself to the age-old adage of mad dogs and Englishmen. The words *'café con leche'* came out of nowhere, though I stumbled and reversed through *'agua potable'*, somehow I managed to get both. Then the one-trick pony-show turned up with an accordion and tambourine. New blood, but the same tired formula. Maybe I'll be in luck and find the town devoid of flamenco marksmen. I felt kind of sorry for the kid on the tambourine as he offered his tool toward me like a beggar, but I had to say no and wave him off. I was not impressed with the budgerigar sound. It's harsh, but fair. They were hardly putting any effort in at all.

I find writing to be a good excuse to keep me occupied when in bars, where previously I have often just sat and stared into space, trying not to be too obvious while eyeing up the local talent. No beer this time either, between the cerveza and the heat, I need a break for a while. The coffee tastes good, and I am feeling relaxed.

It is only May, the place must truly roast in the full heat of summer. Still no English around, of which I am grateful, it gives me a chance to feel that I have escaped home for a while. Which reminds me, I should find an Internet café and let her know all is well. I left on not the best terms after dousing her celebratory night of champagne dinner with my feelings of woe and impending disaster. I just have not been able to get myself right of late. I can't quite grasp what is wrong with me. Maybe it is an age thing. She put me in my place, probably rightly so, as I reeled off somewhat selfishly all the problems that had pushed me into wanting to go off on my own. There has been a month long distance between us, maybe *caused by my own foolishness and sustained by my own regret*, I think they were the words she used. Even so, in as much as one person's solution to rifts is to sweep them away, another's is to face into them and try to resolve the cause. In this, we are opposites. I had to come out here for the break, hopefully to get some perspective.

Anyway, enough of that, it's 7:10 pm and it still is not easing up heat-wise. The last bar cost me four and a half euros for three beers. That's the same price as UK Supermarkets. I don't feel like leaving just yet, and so I order up more coffee and water in my pigeon Spanish. I feel the sun kiss, but I think I timed it right for a first day. I wonder if there are showers in this hostel, and suspect not when you are a roof guest. Then again, I feel that I want to go home after seven days having been cleansed in nothing but sea water. I came out here for a myriad of reasons, and I fancy listing a few right here.

To break my mental chains,
to rough it and see how it feels,
to remember how to hear and follow my inner voice,
to busk,
to let my eye rove free of guilt again,
to see the south-west coast of Spain,
to get a tan,
to learn some Espanol,
to leap into the blue,
to put life in perspective,
to let my dreams expand,
to find direction for my 40's,
to camp, and I mean that in the…
and of course to surf.

Also to meditate, but for that I need to escape the city and the towns, which wont be tonight. I do think I will head for Conil tomorrow, so I need to find out how to get there. It's also time to face the music, I sense the sun will be cooling down soon. If I remember rightly, these Spaniards don't eat until at least 10 pm, so maybe an early nosh for me, to beat the crowds. I haven't eaten since about 10 am English time, so to food, and then a snooze, and then some booze,

One-trick pony

before I strap on the guitar and try to find my troubadourian roots, assuming I have any. Finally the day is upon me. Wow, and oh my god and stuff! I feel a fear and delight so rich I don't know how to feel it correctly. All I know is that I must do it to satisfy some crazy part of me that will regret it forever if I do not do this thing. I have no real idea why it is that way, but it is.

Learning to busk

It's Wednesday. Woke up to find myself in a tent, pitched on top of a roof in the middle of Cadiz. I have vague recollections of doing something with the guitar, and then the rest of the night comes back to me. If you buy beer from the bars here, you actually get a litre bottle, not a pint. That's where it went wrong, or right, depending on how you look at it.

So yesterday was my busking debut, and my first lesson in busking is that no one really pays much attention. Having said that, when I got back to Quo Qadis last night I got requests to play, but I had had enough by then and just wanted to drink. I began the night at twilight on the beach to get a bit of practice, then once I felt warmed up, I walked back in and wandered the town and streets singing and playing as I did so. I also realise that I work best with a sidekick and not alone. When people respond to me, I at first assume they don't like it, so I tend to want to move off which kind of defeats the object. If I had someone with me, I would definitely feel more confident, but as it was I still had fun and I did it, and though the art needs a lot of improvement on my part, I'll do it again. Didn't make any money, but then I wasn't trying to this time. Just trying to get the hang of it.

I wait now for the Internet cafe to open so I can contact the outside world. I am going to head for Conil, it is decided, though I need a camping shop somewhere, as I anticipate El Palmar beach to be void of shops. El Palmar is 3km south from Conil. Lots of walking today. I also heard a bus strike is on, so it may be a long day. No sunburn, so I got that right yesterday. Was fed well at Quo Qadis and enjoyed some good company, though I doubt I'll come back this way. Something is pushing me on.

Is this what traveller's do when in search of themselves? Roam free. I need to make some money busking. Partly because I am overspending on my budget by a half already, and also because I need to know that I could survive on it. Could I make enough of a living

Learning to busk

busking? Certainly not so far. Money from music. That's the connection I have never been able to make with music, and why it saddens me to be denied what feels like my most natural career in life, or should have been. But like for many, it just never worked out. It's always been my passion but never been a money maker. Last night did not inspire financial confidence, and for some reason I am feeling intimidated and quite terrified when busking, yet I have played on stages with bands for years and that never bothers me. It must be the solo thing. So I have to overcome this aspect first and find my confidence out there. A curious paradox - I am desperate to entertain, yet also chronically shy about playing my music. My expectations of it are too high, I know this. I seem to be having terrible anxiety attacks this morning, need to meditate them away, get focused, and get on track. Slept well, so it might have been the rocket fuel coffee this morning that set them off. Think about practicalities instead, and wait for the anxiety to dispel.

I need to get Calor gas for cooking and stock up on some food, and I hope now to find all these in Conil. The town holds 20 thousand people, so I imagine it is well shopped up. Otherwise I may find myself camping on some beach, miles from anywhere, with no food. Conil campsite is 3km from the beach, which is not ideal, I wanted to be on a beach. Not sure what to do about that really.

I also need to take on this busking role more confidently. Stop and play as I go along, maybe. Not quite getting on that track yet, can't say that I am over-excited by the prospect, what does that mean? It is the moment to moment art of survival, that is what I am wanting to learn, instead of just aiming for destinations at planned times. Trying to find *'me'* in the *'here and now'* of it all. It's not easy. And on that note, it feels like it is time to move along.

The fine art of writing

Amazingly, I manage to catch the only bus that is going to Conil today and board it just in time. I best remember to check return bus times when I get there. If I miss the one to Jerez at the end of this trip, then I am going to be fubar and will miss my flight. I can't believe I arrived in time for the bus that leaves at 11 am with just 1 minute left to spare. It rounds off my experience of Cadiz as being one of general difficulty in arriving, but damn easy to get out of once you go with the flow. There is something about travel that awakens this part of you. I had forgotten all about that side of it. Arriving in a place, you pick up on the smallest things. In Cadiz I noticed the wind. Somehow it was tied into that moody drop that I had back at the train station in Cortadura, and then again later on in the afternoon when I headed to the edge of town looking for surf as it hit me and pushed me back. Nothing is familiar when you travel, and something in you tunes in to things you might normally ignore. You start to pay attention to the world around you. I also wonder if a place can want you to leave. There are places I have been that I could not get out of quick enough, and others I have loved from the moment that I set foot in them. We don't often think about the mood of a place being tied into the earth beneath our feet. Cadiz was an odd mixture, I cannot quite decide which way it was swinging for me. I didn't have bad luck here, but I never quite relaxed either. Even so, I think I actually quite like the place. The beach is fantastic and the small streets are charming. The hard yet humorous, and somehow quite passive inhabitants are easy enough to get along with. I felt safe while I was walking about day or night, and it is cheap enough here too.

I haven't been taking photos this trip, I considered it, but then decided to stay focused on the music, just get to busking and playing. I am trying to reconnect with ma geeetar.

Sat on this bus in the first real heat of the day, and I catch a whiff of myself. There was no offer of showers last night, and with the

The fine art of writing

weight of the backpack, I have been sweating quite a bit. I pity anyone who gets too close right now. I have all but become a tramp already. I do regret the contents of the rucksack at the moment, it is really badly weighted and cuts off my breathing in my chest which quickly becomes quite painful and then I get giddy. Can't do anything about it, unfortunately, as the tent and sleeping-bag cause the problem and they are where they are in there, and now it is all locked up below-decks on this single-level coach.

Anyway, the journey continues, and I am wondering what I am headed towards, and what I should try to find there. I have no idea where to go at this point, nor what to expect. I want to camp and find wild seclusion by a beach if I can, but I need food and supermarkets nearby, and also maybe a place to busk that is in walking distance from my tent. I hear that rains are due on Saturday, though I seem to recall the Internet saying it was Thursday. I need to be ready for that. Maybe tonight I could risk a beach sleep, but tomorrow I better be set up and battened down someplace firm. Maybe the bad weather will improve the surf though.

I feel that curious sensation, the one I had before on the plane, that makes me feel like I am headed in the right direction and at the right time. I feel empty but comfortable, and I like it. It brings with it a natural happiness and I smile. Which all the further makes me aware that Cadiz didn't really give me that. I felt a bit serious there.

We pass Cortadura train station again. What an amazingly long and empty beach it has that I can see much better now I am beside it and higher up in a coach. The long stretch of beach is totally free from shops and backed only by the main road. The waves even flatter than yesterday. Anyway, Conil and El Palmar read up as being a bit more surf orientated and with shops that cater to it. Goodbye Cadiz, and thank you for not giving me a harder time. Jesus! I really do stink.

Out into those desolate grassy flats we go. Nice air-con on this bus. The driver very patient with me not understanding that he wanted me to remove my rucksack from my back and put it in the carriage. These people are more patient than I have found elsewhere in Spain. We hit a town, it may be Bahia Sur again. A giant statue rises from it's first roundabout like an iron wall. It is of Africa, and a boat design that

The Road to El Palmar

connects Spain at its southern point to the African continent. I realise how much I have noticed the religion here seems to be Islamic as much as Christian, and there is stuff about Morocco keeps popping up here and there. Maybe I am being drawn to consider going there next. I could check about boats from Tarifa, if I make it there this trip. That gets me on the trail of Paolo Coelho's book, *The Alchemist*. Might not be a bad thing. That book actually inspired me to want to leave work and just go off into the blue yonder for the hell of it.

Of course! *[smacks forehead]* That is when this idea got started! I remember now. The Newquay camping trip with a bunch of friends not long after we all met. Me reading that book on the way back to London afterwards, and wishing I could escape the rat-race but realising I did not any longer know how. That is when this began breaking in me, like those small waves lapping against the beach of Cortadura, but inside me now it is growing and become something of a storm warning. That Newquay trip was two years ago. The Alchemist carries hints of Islam, the Moors, and a source of a power supposedly mightier than Christianity because it is more aware of its roots and it's nature, more aware of it's true identity, and of a man's powerlessness before fate not just a God. I am getting visions of some Arab king descendant, even now immortally ensconced in his tent someplace in North Africa. I am drawn like a moth to the flame of knowledge wherever I find it hidden. I now have a curiosity for Islam that I never had before, though I have seen it's workings in enough of the places that I have been, I even spent a period of time in Jeddah & Riyadh when my Dad was posted out there in my teens. But I can definitely see its influence here in south-west Spain. I was always in awe and respect of it, Arabs had an immense knowledge that they shared with the world, despite our bias view of the Islamic religion. In some ways I have more respect for their history than the Christian religion that was forced upon me at school. The bible was only ever supposed to be for Jews, anyway. I never much liked Christianity. It was too full of flaws. It had no real source of truth, not one that I could see. It was an intellectual invention, and enforced through a demand for a faith upheld by not asking too many questions. It all made very little sense if its believers were willing to be honest about it. What kind of truth is

The fine art of writing

not allowed to be questioned? Jesus in his white robes, blond hair and blue eyes, with flowing locks and beard? Really. Even a kid knows better than that, and you want me to think he is a white man? Nah. He has to be black for starters, and besides that, all monotheistic religions are young, they only go back a few thousand years at best, so what existed before that? Surely that would be far more important for us to know. Yet people freaked out when I asked those kinds of questions. It was obvious to me there was no spirit in Christianity at all, it's been completely bleached out and replaced by a blue-rinse army of confused and desperate old ladies who are afraid of dying, and was completely manipulated to suit the demands of ego-maniacal men in positions of power. God is obviously a man made delusion. I saw through that pretty early on. Man made *god* in his own image, that is how the bible *should* read. In fact that single reversal sums the whole religion up. Islam, on the other hand, is more earthy and fateful somehow. Though it is no better really. The Qu'ran based on interpretations by yet another army of devoted liars, and not only because of the fanatical halfwits who use it as an excuse to abuse others and feel self-justified in doing so. But, I am aware that the roots of Islam go deeper and truer than I at first thought. I am not sure why I know this, maybe because of the strength with which it's less aggressive disciples are able to engage in it. But at the end of the day, all the monotheistic faiths make absolutely no sense unless considered as what they really are, which is tools to control the masses. Population control. I guess it was needed during the last few thousand years as we moved away from pocket-tribes to large habitable cities, but dismissing the polytheistic and animist belief systems was a mistake. We lost direct knowledge of our place in the universe by letting them go. That conversion was most certainly done at the point of a sword, so probably not much choice but to engage in the monotheistic lies and falsified hand-me-downs until they seemed like the only truth around. But they are not the truth - Judaism, Islam, Christianity, are all built on half-truths and lies. Give me animist beliefs any day.

That's the world put to rights, and it really probably is that simple. So, now where am I? Another town someplace. I was not paying attention. It just dawned on me that the bus was three and a half euros,

The Road to El Palmar

which is something like three English pounds for a 70km journey. Damn, I am hungry again and craving a cigarette. There are a couple of other things I wanted to address on this trip that I forgot to add to my list - I wanted to lose a bit of the belly fat, and replace smoking with a bit of inner peace. Addictions can be so difficult to reign in, I never succeeded with stopping smoking, though I have tried.

We pick up a few more passengers, and I notice the architecture is changing again. More domed roofs, and Persian arches. I knew I was seeing Islamic influences around here and now that confirms it. I guess it's not all that far south from here to Africa and the Moors country.

I always avoided taking coaches anywhere, but I have to say that I am really enjoying this one. Comfortable, roomy, only a few people, and a good view, plus it is nicely air-conditioned. I think that town was Chiclerana that we just went through. The land now looks more like England in summer time. The same rise and fall of undulating hills all interspersed with semi-woodland and fields growing…er…some green stuff.

Conil 15km. It's been an hour so far. I really think I will have to get a pipe for pondering. I am also starting to realise that I should not think about what I write and whether it would interest anyone, otherwise I probably wouldn't bother writing at all. Someone said that travel writers should not write about themselves, but I am not totally convinced of that, sometimes I think it is the interaction of the outside with the inside that is the story. I have a lot of stories I would like to tell. I guess the balance is found by avoiding egotistical narcissism while knowing what accessible topic will entertain generically. It's much the same with music, trying to find the right twang on the strings to resonate with the most number of listeners. I also think it is probably best not thought about too much, otherwise it will become like music has for me - something I try to do to please people, or to succeed with it in some way. As a result I have now forgotten how to do it *just for the love of it*. This is true, and in part why I chose to come out here with my guitar, trying to get to know it again. I have been so busy with corporate living the last few years that I have let the music fall away, and I miss it. But writing is a relatively new art for me, and writing while travelling certainly is. I have been writing lots of random

The fine art of writing

stuff since I was a teenager, but I mostly turned it into song lyrics or left it as rhyming poetry, until a few years ago when the writing became more manic. But there is no real aim with my writing, it is just an outlet, and in that way so far remains untainted. I write to let whatever is inside me, come out. That is my style, I guess. That makes it an exorcism of sorts too, or maybe when it's good it is almost a kind of divination. As I write, I can feel that something unlocks inside me, and that allows a flow to begin, that then leads me into areas of thought, or perception, or feeling, that I would not have reached otherwise. In this way, I find writing is capable of being a valuable and almost magical act, or could be considered so because it has the potential to change ones mood and emotional state. For the reader, I have no idea, but for me, definitely true. The art of writing, to me, is not the structured skill-set taught in English classes, but rather the fine art of mastering how to use lyrical dexterity to change things. Could writing lead to evolution of the mind? I think so. Music certainly does. I have felt that change myself, for example after listening to Pink Floyd for the first time, it was a perfect example of the impact of music to completely change a person's direction in life. It was like having a new wisdom poured into me via my ears, it was an immediate revolution and something in me found traction in it. I felt it happen as it changed me, but I digress...with writing it is the energy in the content that matters, in my opinion anyway. It is more about what it carries inside the words, between the words, and not the text or grammatical correctness that is of primary importance. That is my take on it, such as it is, being the unpublished, unknown, barely got started, expert on writing. Anyway, got to pay attention now, I think I am arriving at Conil.

The white walls of Conil

Conil, I like straight away. A more Spanish feel to it. White painted buildings, and the people here seem super friendly and laid back too. It is set on a slight incline that flows up and away from a long sandy beach which you can't see until you happen upon it by walking through the thin, bright-white alleys of the town. It's all very closed in, but in a quaint way, not too claustrophobic, rather more like a village feel, and it is calm compared to the more large-town energy of Cadiz.

I stop at a beach-front bar, totally out of breath and feint from the ten minute walk down from the bus stop. I have to do something about my rucksack, which is putting a bad stress on my chest and heart, knocking me out every few minutes. I still haven't recovered as I write this.

This town seems expensive. Seven euros for a plate of calamari on the menu here. There also seem to be lots of rich looking German tourists milling about along the beach front. Not my favourite creature, I find they can be quite rude. And sure enough, moments later I am given a barely hidden look of disdain by the barman who clearly has airs and graces. Hmm. I now suspect there will be some snobbery in Conil. Maybe it is just on the tourism end of it. Don't judge too harshly, yet. I guess I don't look like the right sort, and that may actually be a fair assessment.

I am unsure what to do next. It is coming up to 1 pm, and I can't walk far with this bloody heavy rucksack. Saw a map back there in the street, but no clues on it. Signs for camping led out of town. Felt like Clint Eastwood as I arrived in town, caught reflection of myself again as bus drove off, guitar in my hand looked like a rifle. Tumbleweeds rolling through the streets. The wind is merciless again, nearly took me off my feet as I reached the beach. Again, I have the odd feeling that it seems to want to tell me to go elsewhere. The wind is blowing me on.

Christ! I still feel feint. This is not good. I notice that I have lost a ring from off my finger. I guess it was time for it to go. Has been

The white walls of Conil

falling off my finger ever since L left my place of work. She was with me when I bought it, she was my compadre at work and now she is gone out my life. Gone and got married, moved to the Lakes, up north. Now the ring too, gone on someplace. Sometimes these things have their time in your life, and then they move on. People, places, things, and rings. It's natural, and we should figure how to let them go. Something comes to replace it just as naturally too. Nature abhors a vacuum, after all. I also know this is a time of endings for me and a time to start clearing what I no longer need away, getting ready for new beginnings.

I still feel feint. Damn that rucksack! A leggy, model-quality woman goes by. Forgot they existed. This town must be dripping in rich people and that confirms it. I thought I could smell money here. I really have absolutely no class whatsoever at the moment. I stink. The barmen knows it too. Looking tardy and messed-up is going to win me no favours here. The look of the traveller serves only to outcast him. That is the one side of it that I don't like. People can be so damn fickle. He is thought of as a beggar, and *that* I am not. Or am I?

Anyway, it's time I thought of what the hell to do with myself. Noticing how important decisions are now. Trying to gauge whether to go left or right at a turning is a decision that could end up costing me a week in disasters, or lead me on to perfection and paradise. How do I decide? This is where I wanted to be, to learn how to *read the signs* again. Do I go this way, or do I go that way? How to decide? No idea what lies in either direction, but I know what I need, and it forms like a wish or request to the gods. I lay it out to the world, to the universe to guide me, and then keep my eyes peeled for the signal that it might give back. The wind didn't want me on the beach, but I came down here anyway. What do I need? Well, I guess what I need is to find a camping place, or at least somewhere to lock up my stuff while I hunt down a sleeping spot for tonight. I may be in the rough tonight. Gawd. I hope the rains don't come early. So much to learn, so many opportunities to make big and regrettable mistakes.

Lesson two: efficiency

After leaving the beach bar, I headed back into town and was nearly passing out with the weight of the rucksack pulling against the top of my chest. It sounds pathetic, I know, but somehow I have packed it really top heavy. The effect is, that it does something weird to my chest and that literally knocks me out. I think the heart can't pump or something. Potential crisis. I was having major problems staying coherent in this heat.

I eventually find my way through what is essentially a labyrinth of white walls, it is like a damn maze here. The only way is by compass, I swear, and everything seems to be uphill to boot. So I eventually happen, by luck, upon the exact spot that the bus dropped me off. I notice at this point what I should have noticed before, a large sign saying - *'YOU ARE HERE'*, and a map on a billboard in the middle of the street. A quick check, and I find *Tourismo Informatica* and it is…the very door next to the signpost that I am currently looking at. What a dick-head! Did I learn nothing yesterday at Cortadura?

I enter in, and learn all I need in English from the ladies inside. Taxis, bus timetables, camping spots, and shops. They give me a map with all these items circled, and off I go like a hound after the rabbit once again. I start off at an excited trot, but before long I find myself dying from cardiac arrest once more and realise that despite my map, I am again completely lost. Finding a landmark, it dawns on me that the map is at some kind of scale, and I have over-shot the taxi point by about half a kilometre.

DID I LEARN NOTHING HERE TODAY!

I traipse painfully back to the beginning, and just as I locate the taxi point, a little old lady accosts me. From what I can make out she is offering me an apartment for 20 euros a night. I have visions of her tippy-toeing in at two in the morning and demanding sexual gratification, or maybe battering me over the head, or something sinister and done in Spanish. You know how the mind works when gift

Lesson two: efficiency

horses trot up unexpectedly.

'Gracias, but no.' I say to her resolutely, and then I walk on.

Hang on! Did I learn nothing here today?

Yes, maybe finally I did, and I waddle back in a condition that is more befitting of her age than mine, only to find her in a bar and offering the same thing to two female travellers. The same ones, it turns out, that I had just been chatting to by the signpost at the start, but whom I also already know to be leaving Conil today. I announce to the craggy old wench that I have changed my mind. She pulls a face, but getting nowhere with the ladies, decides to take me on.

As we walk back to where her apartment is, and those demonic fears come galloping into my brain once again, I realise that finally I have actually taken the opportunity as it presented itself to me. This is a landmark moment, and should really be marked down in my journal as the day I overcame some ingrained British sense of reservation. I actually acted on a situation, rather than just watched it go by. I could elaborate on this, but given it was a first, I will wait until I have mastered it a bit better, assuming that I ever do. Suffice to say, I followed her to the door of the place she had in mind. Maria then let us in.

Maria was the housemaid or maybe the real owner, I don't rightly know, but Maria then showed me around the rest of it. By this time, unsurprisingly, the price had gone up, and it was also now for two nights minimum stay. I knew that I wasn't going to take it, those galloping demons had become ferocious wildebeest when I met Maria. She was nice enough, but had the look of a hatchet queen. But I didn't care. I said my thank-yous, or rather my *grassy-asses*, and then made excellent use of my lack of communication skills to achieve the one thing that I was certainly adept at, I obfuscated everything in pigeon Iglesias and then quickly legged it.

Somewhere up the road I re-discovered the taxi rank and got into one. I then headed for camp Fuente de Gallo. It cost seven euros and was driven by El Guapo via a camping supply shop that was closed. Damn. But as soon as I arrived at Fuente, things started to look a lot better. The young, bright, and friendly gent on the desk was chatty, and his English was good. I learnt about the three or four day sou'wester that blows out to sea, and that should break any day now. I learnt that El Palmar was good for surf. I learnt the local beach points, and where to pitch my tent in Fuente's campsite. The bar, the supermarket. It all fell into place. It was time for me to pitch and go.

So what have I learnt today? A traveller needs *efficiency*. Naff as that sounds, I need to learn efficient use of my energy. I am now starting to feel how each meal gives me enough energy for X amount of time. This is good. When you bring your life down to that level, then you are definitely living in a more natural and moment-to-moment way. I have been too busy to crave food. Not like I would do back in the UK, eating just out of boredom more than anything. This is the first epiphany, and it may be a key thing to note about trying to get back to basics.

The next problem you face is *stupidity*. Stupid decisions that get made in haste and panic. That is pretty much the norm for me back in London, and a terrible habit that I have become attached to. London is fast-paced, and you don't have the luxury of time to ponder things. Up until I met the little old lady back there in Conil, I had been functioning mostly in a traditionally British mode. It is hard to shake it. We don't really talk to strangers unless we want their country. I didn't used to be this way, so it only took three goes for me to recall another way of being. Any true Brit who reads this might be aware of it, or might not, but it is an inherent part of our culture to be like it. We are reserved and stand-offish, and we are judgemental. I think it is out of a fear of strangers. But whatever it's roots, it is just something in our cultural upbringing and not a fault *per se*. Having said that, it probably goes a long way to explain why we are perceived as being distant and difficult. We Brits have a natural ability to sit and wait for things to come to us, then when they do, we do nothing. Rather, we then expect them to engage us first, and not the other way around. We have an aloofness and apathy that does us no favours, not really. It's not good enough out here, and it certainly doesn't work when travelling. I have noticed it. It is a part of me that I associate with being British, and I need to drop it to function better.

So, back to the *efficiency* aspect. This is important because I need to

Lesson two: efficiency

stop wandering around in towns looking lost, especially when the map is at the very place that I started out from. There is also a *trust* that goes with *efficiency*. Trust fate to dump you in pastures full of auspicious potential. Around you will likely be all the things you need, if you can just pay attention. Fate often lands us quite well, especially if we actually bother to slow down and look around. So when surroundings are unfamiliar, rather than panic and run as I have been, instead I need to just stop. Freeze still, and look around. Then, as soon as the merry-go-round begins to slow down, I may just find what I need or the start of the path towards it. The clues for me, in this regard, are in the last two days of activity and occasional success. I am now tented up in a nice place and ready to explore, and hopefully to progress on from here and a little more smoothly than I have thus far.

So, with the afternoon weather still hot and looking delightful, I left the campsite and wandered like a merry minstrel alone with my guitar. Just a wandering troubadour, if you will. I soon found myself walking along high cliff-tops above the ocean, no one was around. I sang out to sea, and I sang as I strolled, and it all felt very good.

It seems I am now in a hilly, virtually beach-less and somewhat rocky countryside. Lots of building work is going on. Huge apartment villas here. This place will explode with tourism soon and someone knows it. After leaving Conil in the taxi earlier, we drove past rich looking villas and then onto a dust road. This place is happening now, and it is being prepared. Maybe this less developed side of Spain could end up becoming the next Costa del Sol, but for now, it is mine. There are very few people at the campsite, hardly anyone in fact. Though I find it a bit pricey at eight euros just to pitch a tent for one night, it's cheaper than the alternative down at Maria's. I am now off to try to catch the bus to Conil, to see what I can find there. It goes from the Hotel Flamenco, apparently.

Eventually my paean ambulation takes me past the Hotel Flamenco, so I wander in. I meet two old dears in the lobby, they are very English. Seems that they aren't too impressed with the place and one of them, who seems to think she is the Queen, clearly isn't too impressed with me either. She scowls at me and is reserved and distant.

The Road to El Palmar

I decide to ignore her attitude. As we wait for the bus I am a little tipsy still from a sneaky drink or two in the bar, and I am now somewhat more chatty. So I give it my best Dickie Burton accent and soon it seems to win them over. In fact I struggle to shake them once we reach Conil. I eventually manage it, and not long after I do, a mini disaster befalls me. I break a string. Top E. It just snaps. Drama. I have got a spare set, but it's back at the tent, so this isn't good for busking. I find a shop, but this is the land of flamenco and everything is made of nylon. I need steel. After waiting in a queue at the local wool shop, of all places, I get a nylon string as a temporary replacement. Wool shops, is where they sell guitar strings, obviously. But nylon-only. This is an issue for me. Nylon plays a lot quieter. I am done for. Oh well. I go for a wander.

At some point I find myself playing a lower key, one-string-down version of a popular British song in an empty side street. I can't quite work out the chorus in this key. I spot an Internet cafe as I wander, and then spot Hotel Oasis. Funny that, the song that I was just murdering was by the band called Oasis. The wind has dropped now, and the first clouds of my holiday start to blanket over a portion of the sky to the north-west. The sun is not as hot as it was yesterday. It's 7 pm, and the last bus back to my campsite leaves in one hour.

I enjoy some time down by the beach in a bar there. Sink a couple more lagers. It takes a few goes to order them as my 'cerveza' had become too Spanish even for the Spaniards to comprehend. I was starting to sound more like Sylvester the cat but with an even worse lisp. The bar girl puts me right on my pronunciations. It does actually start with a 'C' and not with a 'thssfffwww' . You learn this stuff as you go along.

Two more Germans cruise into the bar. I am now at the south end of the beach in Bar Bahia. I have lost my 6th string and the town doesn't sell metal strings, only nylon ones. I am limping with my guitar licks. Is this time to move back to nylon again? Maybe it is. But how the hell will it be heard without an amp? A woman sits down with the two guys. Well, boys. They have all sat down right by me. I can hold no responsibility for my actions at this time of broken silver and too much beer. The guitar felt like a gun in my hand today, as I wandered

Lesson two: efficiency

lonely as a star. For some reason I notice that the woman with them has very thin wrists, they seem too thin for the rest of her.

Two cars go by. Tunes pumping out. Loud and obnoxious it invades the moment, reminds me of Uxbridge boy-racers of which there are far too many. All trainers, baseball hats, loud music and aggression, and that package often comes dressed in Burberry. This must be the Spanish version of that. One of the boys in the car has a white streak bleached through his hair. It is everywhere these days. Attention-seeking behaviour in the youth. I blame satellite and MTV for the unification and synthesis of this somewhat crass global phenomena. They go past, and the music fades in a Doppler effect, but the *thump-thump-thumpety-thump* of their noise pollution carries on for a longer time until finally it fades away into the distance. Everyone gets back to what they were doing. Attention-seeking works, I guess.

The discussion of rain comes up between various tables in the bar. There is spit falling out of clear blue skies. I have witnessed this before. It is in the realm of locusts, frogs, and pitchforks, and it makes no sense to try to interpret it. The conversation stops as quickly as the spit started.

Yet another car that sails past loudly. This time with MOS tunes blaring from it. I feel like I am in Ibiza, maybe we should all get up and start throwing shapes. Once again, it is time for me to consider my options. It is 30 minutes to the bus leaving. I am now feeling a bit drunk. Should I stay here and get totally blind drunk, or should I go and get the bus? My broken string, and the fact there is a bar at the campsite, tells me that maybe I should leave. But these cars going by that are pumping tunes, it suggests excitement is to be found here, but I am not sure why it should really suggest that, nor if I would much like the excitement I might, or might not, find.

More spit falls from clear skies. I am a man lost in space and time. Walking to the toilet, I realise I am much more drunk than I thought. I should probably have had a proper meal first. Never mind. Checking myself in the mirror, I see that I am ageing. There is a humour in that, but I fail to find it. Somehow age is terrifying, I am not sure why. It should be glorious. Maybe it is because it brings with it a sense of powerlessness. Maybe that is why I drink. Alcoholic oblivion is mine to own. I can still manage a smile. Ooh, maybe don't do that. That word reads like *mango* as I write this, but I did mean *manage*, okay here we go, south and down.

The first letter of the alphabet must have been the hardest one to invent, and it is devastating when left out, or when you make an *e* look like an *o*. Took me a while to figure out what I wrote. Wars have been waged for less, no doubt. I need food. Where can I eat? What shall I do? Think fast, but thinking drunk like a skunk. Yesh. If I stay, I best figure out the cabs and how long they hang about, elsh I'll be stranded with a long walk, and I have no idea which way to walk. It would be dark by the time I walked it, possible opportunity for death. Probably fall off a cliff. No problem. My neighbouring tables gets up and leaves as I write this. We nod good bye, the rain conversation having briefly bonded us but none of us could find anything more to talk about.

The spit continues to fall some more. The town of Conil is actually relatively quiet when hoodlums are not driving around it. I think I must move. Head towards the epicentre and decide from there. God, is this who I am now?

I find the bus waiting, and I loiter around in the last of the day's sunshine that has remained despite the threat of rain and the curious cloudless spitting. I lightly strum my five stringed, limping guitar. Though it is me that's limping now. Limping through life. The bus driver seems animated, and then introduces me to a local bar manager. He reminds me of a carpenter friend from back home. Apparently he has an amigo who can fix my guitar tomorrow night for me, metal strings no problem. I say that I will return. A drunk that he was chatting to, or should I say *another* drunk that he was chatting to, offers me some nylon string from his pocket. Actual string. You know. Funny guy. We all laugh heartily, and then go on our way.

I feel deflated. Don't know why. Find myself thinking I do more writing in this journal than playing of the guitar. I don't know why that makes me sad, but it does. I strum the guitar gently as the bus bounces around, kind of like a man might fondly stroke his dying pet dog. I am dropped off by the bus driver, his only passenger that evening. I make my walk back into the campsite and find the restaurant open, so I

Lesson two: efficiency

order some food. Finally, I get to eat properly today. Now I feel on the wrong side of the alcohol. Wide-awake and coherent, until I try to actually function then it all goes wrong. *Is this who I am now?*

Next, I suddenly feel inexplicably horny, and assume it is the effect of the sun. Food arrives. It's as close to a proper meal as I have had in the two days that I have been here, but it costs me the better part of eight Euros. This Conil place sure is expensive. I pour oil and salt on it like it's…what is this now? I thought that was the main dish, then the next one turns up. Okay then. Eight euros goes a lot further than I thought.

I am now stuffed and ready to sleep. It's been a long day. I have had enough of it. That old familiar sadness lingers in the background awaiting my participation. Probably why I get drunk, and almost definitely partially caused by it. I feel torn between an intense sense of loneliness and the need to find a way to let go and enjoy my life. This is my special moment of freedom, and I am not sure that I am making the most of it, nor in the best way possible. We can eat, smoke, and drink ourselves into oblivion. In fact I often do. We all do whatever we do, but at the end of it all, there is always that damn lonely pain. Always, that same incredible sadness is there. I don't know when I first noticed it. It was there already, waiting for me to show up, maybe simply because I exist. Do you get that too? Come on. I think you do. I think we all cover it up and try to hide it. We get busy to numb it, and we seek out company so we don't have to feel it. I saw it in the eyes of my dying grandfather, and also in the foul and vile gasp of a drunk that I once tried to help as he collapsed unconscious to the floor of a shopping centre. I taste that sadness every single goddamn day. What is it? Is it prevalent in me because I tried to look it in the eye? I think once you do that kind of thing, you can never escape it's glare.

Melodramatic as this all may sound, that loneliness and anxiety seems to increase with knowledge and awareness and as time goes by. It develops more as we start to acknowledge just where we are, and just what is going on here, and what is coming. Ends are coming, always endings. It seems to me sometimes, that the earth is just some kind of a prison planet. That the things we can't see, nor seem to work

The Road to El Palmar

out about our emotional states, are that way mostly because we would not handle the truth if we saw what is behind it all. Better to remain dumb, if there is no escape, or if really we are slaves to something we could not face seeing. But that sadness, that ache, that eternal anxiety. It is like a pressure, it actually kills the joy of life. Squashes it flat. Takes it apart. Explodes it, from the inside out. Only the strong survive, and ultimately even they don't. It is in the eye of a setting sun, as the last rays of the day begin to weaken, then I can sense it flavoured in nostalgia. As soporific night falls to help us forget, we drink, and we dance, and we try to blot out the memories of our pain. As if the truth no longer exists for us when we are numb to it. And I thought for a long time that sex was the answer, a cure for that endless anxiety that I felt trapped in. I thought sex was the secret with which we might beat the bastard back. Now, I don't think so. We are simply victims of the universe, it's children, but it's victims too. We cannot change the universe at all, though we think we can, it's laws never change. Maybe that is the point. We must eventually die, become extinct, and this is just a fact to be faced. Sex is just a trick of Nature, to get us to do her bidding, but it certainly helps with my anxiety when I get struck down by it. At first it works, but not permanently. It soon swings back the other way again not long afterwards. Sex is a bit tricky, it drives us with a hope, and we use it to seal our relationships. Hope for connection, for maybe a child, or for love, or even just for sex. Sex promises us freedom from the pain, promises a moment of ecstatic divinity, or unity, or just a promise that there is something, or someone, out there for us, that there is someone who just might give a shit. But sex is a liar.

I am drunk, and I am literally now dribbling onto this book. I will find no answers by doing this, but I am driven to try all the same. Time to hole up for the night, and see what drifts to me in sleep. And what drifted to me in sleep, was this...

What do I have to give you?
All that I had, I have given away.
I let myself go, I let myself down.
My future body lies cold somewhere in an unmarked grave.

Lesson two: efficiency

*Like a soldier of freedom that no one ever knew,
nor cared that he was a child of the stars.
They all rise, and they all fall.
Another lost angel, fell down from paradise,
just to say 'hello', but you did not notice him there.
What do I have to give you?
Just a kiss, and a wish upon your way.
You want to know what it looks like in paradise?
Maybe one day we will know.*

What's freedom anyway?

Last night I dreamed of heaven, in the cold light of day I see I was a fool
I stole into the room of a young virgin, and though paradise was mine, I broke the rules.
Seven gates of hell were torn asunder, and now my neck's upon la guillotine.
For the pleasures to be had from rape and plunder, are the reserved prerogative of kings and queens.
And all the world's hatred poured upon me, because I had done what they had only wished to do.
But hated themselves to find the panther, loose within their souls and hunting too.
Last night I dreamed of heaven, but in my fear it woke me to a state of hell,
because the twisted need for lustful satisfaction lives on in me, the reasons for which, I can not tell.

Its 3 am. This morning the wind seems to have picked up again, and though it appears I chose a good spot, on a slope under a thick foliage canopy, the treetops around the campsite suggest there is a hurricane going on. It sounds like the angry roar of muffled jet planes as it storms randomly across the skies above me, ripping and whipping ferociously at the sides of of my tent.

I dreamed that I was with some woman, I have no idea who she was. I was throttling a young pock-faced teenager, accusing him of calling me something. He was denying it, and was about to retaliate with disastrous consequences, when I awoke with an odd sensation, a spike of pain in my solar-plexus that still lingers now.

Tomorrow will be my third day out, and I still have not had the courage to do the things I should. Tai-chi exercises in the morning regardless of who is around, for example. And I have not played and sung properly in public yet, not really. I play when people are not around. Hmm. Tomorrow I must do this second item at the very least, and here in Conil. Set myself up on a boardwalk, or in a bar if one will

What's freedom anyway?

have me, and just play. God damn it, I must get over this fear! There are no other buskers here in town, but I did catch some kids laughing at me at one point. People also say something that I don't understand, as I wander past them quickly while strumming away. I am trying to find a way to break the ice on my fear of having an audience. I keep thinking that they are used to the high-class skills of flamenco artists, and I must seem like some amateur idiot to them. I have to let myself off a bit, since my live work to date has only ever been on a stage with the backdrop of a loud rock and roll band. Maybe that explains my difficulty in overcoming this immense wall of embarrassment that I am facing. It is just so odd, and such an internal conflict.

What is that now? Ah-ha. I am sun burnt on my shoulders, my arms and worst of all, my lips. I need the servicio and to stretch my limbs a bit. I poke my head out of my small tent. The wind whips the air as I do. I feel a tension that I cant explain, again. It seems so angry out there tonight, but at least no rain. I am hallucinating figures, maybe murderers lurk in the flashes of the shadows created by the streetlights that adorn the campsite paths, while the trees thrash about with that monstrous wind adding effect. But there are no clouds either, I see. And there is Scorpio high in the eastern sky, it is the only constellation I can see from here, how funny, and of course that is my birth sign. Maybe this is that moment of a death and rebirth that I felt I was headed towards. The scene from my tent door holds a certain dramatic quality, with the Scorpio constellation as the backdrop. A tree sways and glitters under the lamp of what could be an old English street light, beneath which I really should be playing Romeo and Juliet right now, that would actually set the scene out there perfectly. I should also try to sleep some more, so that I am fresh for tomorrow. Time to make for the *servicio* and then try for more sleep.

I awake again at 7:30 am and to another sunny day. The wind seems to have dropped off a bit now, and I realise that one blessing of the wind is that there are no mosquitoes. Of course, I spot one within seconds of having the thought. I watch the ground outside of my tent for a while as I adjust somewhat painfully to being awake. The solid ground has given me aches and light bruising, something I will need to

The Road to El Palmar

address before I sleep again. I did not bring a mattress, just a sleeping bag. There are snails, spiders, and woodlice all milling about and trundling to and fro. It is hypnotic to watch this miniature city of *Insectia*. I guess to them we are much like dinosaurs, and they will undoubtedly still be here long after some Apocalyptic drama claims our species. Only the small survive, it's a numbers game. I am drawn to wonder about Darwin's theories of evolution and really can't see how minute bacteria ever evolved into something like a brontosaurus. But then how else did life arrive on earth? From plumes beneath the ocean or from outer space? And how come man hasn't evolved or adapted further in any other way than his colour and hairlessness throughout the six million or so years he has been here? It makes no sense. All I can do is leave it at that. Bringing more relevant matters into focus, I decide that today I will take a shower.

I stand before the mirror in the shower block. I really need to find a way to thin down my hair a bit. I seem to have decided to grow it after my last experience in a hair salon where I was left nursing a bleeding cheekbone from a misplaced set of scissors. I couldn't believe the owner had the gall to ask for full payment after that, as I stood there helpless, dripping blood from a gash on my face that began to splatter onto her desk. Incredulous, wounded, shocked, I paid the money. I knew she would dock the hairdresser's wage otherwise, and I felt a bit sorry for the poor young lass. She had immediately run off into the back room crying. I never went back there again, and it gave me more fear of hairdressers than I already had. I dated two salon owners, though neither of them ever tried to stab me, they probably thought about it at some point.

Today I have thick and matted hair, made thicker by salt in the air I guess. Frankly, I look zany. After a wash I may look like one of the hair-bear bunch. I may try leaving some conditioner in to calm it all down, but these experiments often go wrong. Come to think of it, I need to wash my t-shirt and shirt too. I have only a jumper to wear while I am waiting for them to dry, but the day is beginning to warm and once the sun rises above the tree-line to the south of my tent, I don't think it will take long.

The campsite is well decked out, with wonderfully hot showers

What's freedom anyway?

and drinkable water. And the bar opens in half an hour, which is a bit tempting. I am thinking today I will do a reconnaissance to El Palmar and back. See if the surf scene is there, and if it is, then go along tomorrow with my tent and pitch up somewhere. Otherwise, stick it out here in Conil for a few days.

I briefly return to my tent and open my sleeping bag to eject some sand and let it air. Then I hang my pants on the zipper of the door, in part to ward off predators, then head back to the shower block, there is still no one around the camp site at all.

Typically, I wash my t-shirt and have a fantastic shower only to find it now clouding over, so how can I dry it? Lucky I only washed that, and not my only other garment, the sleeved shirt. While I wait to see if it will dry, I re-string my guitar with an 11 gauge Ernie Ball that I somehow thought to bring with me. I only change the one string, knowing that if I break any more then I will have to use the others, even though the sizing will be wrong. Feels good to have it back in action, and I play a while, writing a new tune. I think I will name this guitar *Jacqueline*. It seems like a female. I feel that resonance beginning to awaken between myself and the guitar again. It's been more than ten years since I felt that. Back when I used to play every day, sometimes all day. Now I play once a week, if that. My dreams of rock and roll have faded with it, though I suppose it is good I kept my hand in these years. Clouds definitely coming on strong above me. Then a sudden gust of wind puts my wet t-shirt into the dirt. Damn it. They are looking like rain clouds too. I may yet be stranded for a time here on campus. Not many people about still, could be time to meditate, then to get some breakfast in and see which way the day is going to swing. I juggle stuff about in my one-man tent a bit, realising if it rains in this wind, then it is sure to leak with the sides touching things, so I move what I can to the centre.

I tried to do some healing-hands on myself last night. I had a wrist-pull that is now gone. Maybe that shiz works. I'm trying to think of ways that I could make money other than busking, not that I have stayed put long enough to make any so far, but it would be nice to travel around like this for a few years. Get out of that damn rat-race. Minimise. Find a way to free-style again but earn it somehow, not just

The Road to El Palmar

blagging hand-outs off the Government. Somehow it must be possible without becoming a slave to yet another hamster-wheel. Carrying round a massive rucksack would suck, mind you. Is it possible to jettison everything? Everything except a cash-card, if you had enough cash in the account I suppose you could. That would be good. But that requires being rich in the first place, the point is to achieve this idealism from a condition of poverty - the zero cash line. Those essential survival-needs always in focus: *shelter, water, fire, food, survival skills, company*. You can't avoid needing them. *Air* is in there too really, but for this exercise let's assume it is available, safe to breathe, and still comes for free. I would have to lose the rucksack, but I could not afford to rent rooms. What am I going to do, live up a tree? Hmm.

I really don't think I could rough it, just not my style for long periods of time. Five day festivals is one thing, coming out here for a week is one thing, but living like it is another. So maybe the idea is dead before it even begins. Besides, I do have a mortgage back home, and other debts which wont be paid of until at least 2007, and a career, and a girlfriend, and no doubt I will have accrued even more debts and ties before I pay other ones off. But this is part of what I am out here to think about and to consider. I need to re-discover a sense of freedom that I have lost. I came out here to get a taste of that reality again, and to consider just how I would cope if I went for it, gave everything up and started to travel.

What could I do to survive footloose and free? How would I afford to travel? It's hard if you don't take the opportunity when you are younger, and freer, and maybe a bit more stoopider too. I enjoyed freedom for a long time in my yoof, but by the age of 27 I was suffering from it, and I had to get into the rat-race for my sense of sanity if nothing else. Am I too old now, ten years on? Nah, I am still stupid enough, but not really young enough to kid myself about it all anymore. Maybe this is my last hurrah, who knows. Oh, how desperate that sounds! Back then I was too busy visiting other planets to care much about travel beyond the room I was in, and there were plenty of adventures to be found in the back of ones eyelids on the right kind of cocktail. It's only the last year that has seen me lessen my recreational drug intake and begin to seriously consider life outside of my inner,

What's freedom anyway?

hallucinatory universe. I did not have much choice after getting involved in a mortgage, there was not much money left over for such mayhem and frivolity each week. I had to cut it all back. Not to mention the state it was all starting to leave me in. The come-downs only ever get worse with time, and the highs become less and less appealing. I don't think anyone looks good taking drugs much after 40 years old. I have had my ups and downs with the drugs, and I do wonder how my heart can really be expected to keep me going for another 40 years, but its not unreasonable to think it might, especially if I replace drugs with more healthy substitutes.

So, finally, I have begun to do exactly that, and now most days attempt yoga, Tai-chi and, of course, meditation. All of which will take a long time to learn. It is how they work, by gradually tuning the body, soul, and mind towards better ways, or so I am told. So the battle to resist just getting off of my head has now become the front-line of my life, and a battle certainly rages there, as it always has. A battle for knowledge and understanding, as much a cure for boredom. All the while trying to avoid the pitfalls, pains, addictions and miseries that come with it.

Maybe I should learn to just enjoy being here, enjoy the rat-race, enjoy the mortgage, enjoy the routine, but for some of us we are born with that nagging feeling that there is something more to all this. If there is an answer, it is already within us, I guess. What is freedom anyway? I seem to long for it, but don't even really know what it means. But I realise I need to find more healthy ways than I have been living, and I *am* trying to figure that out.

Though right now, I cant even figure out how to make a buck from busking, so I can't very well hope to crack open the secrets of the universe. It is a defiantly ordinary and boring world at times, despite being so mysterious and inexplicable to defy definition. In the end, it is really just about surviving, and in the midst of that, trying to rinse a bit of happiness from it all along the way. And on that note, I finish up my morning coffee and see that the sun once again shines out there. Those clouds that were threatening have lifted. It is time for my day to begin. I guess this *is* my moment of freedom, brief but beautiful.

Meditation classes for the rich

I fear that a long walk lies ahead of me today. 10 miles each way at least. I need to reach El Palmar and see if surf potential is there, and if not, then return to camp. I will travel light, not even my guitar, and I need to keep my eyes open for opportunity to speed my journey time, else I may lose the entire day to wrong decisions. Now it is time to put into action what I should have learnt yesterday. Decision making is all about opportunity and seeing it around me. Efficiency and trust. Here I go. I wish me luck!

I discover that I have an hour to wait before the bus will arrive at Hotel Flamenco to take me into Conil. I plan to meditate at the bus-stop, but then decide to check out the hotel. I enter in through the posh lobby and ask at the desk what time the bus is due. I already know it is due at 12:30 pm. I look better today with washed, trainers, clean white shirt, and for that extra touch my jumper over my shoulders and loosely tied by the arms around my neck. I think I look sporty enough.

First off, speak to the most senior looking person in the place. This immediately stops any lesser personnel daring to talk to you. It is the nature of hierarchy that a subordinate does not be seen to question the act of a manager, therefore in talking to *him*, you are instantly above approach from any lesser minion. Also making the question low-key but snappy, as if with an air of someone on a schedule who knows where he is going. You will, most times, also present the manager with an illusion he is talking to a guest. Why else would someone appear so at ease, yet quietly going somewhere and in need of an immediate answer to a simple question?

Holding an erect posture and a firm, yet light but determined gait, I glide into the lobby as if I own the place. In this way the manager does not bat an eyelid when, instead of exiting after our brief rapport, I head deeper into the hotel. I want to take a gander. Seems to work, I

Meditation classes for the rich

am through, and I now have the hotel to look at. Not interested really, but I swing by the pool and discover a track running down to a beach. It is the hotel's secret beach. Bloody hell! It's at least a mile long, and absolutely gorgeous. I will be back, if I remain in Fuente del Gallo.

Down at the beach, I sit and draw a picture into my notebook, drawing is something I never have had time for before. It's not art, but it is mine. I then meditate for an hour by the steps on the beach. It is very pleasant here. Couples go to and fro. Some people sit down nearby, and they then appear to become very still and meditative, maybe inspired by my calm refrain. *Meditation classes for the rich.* That could be a cushy number, while giving me time in the day to practice an art I enjoy. Food for thought. Now the bus is due. Meditation class is over for the morning, folks.

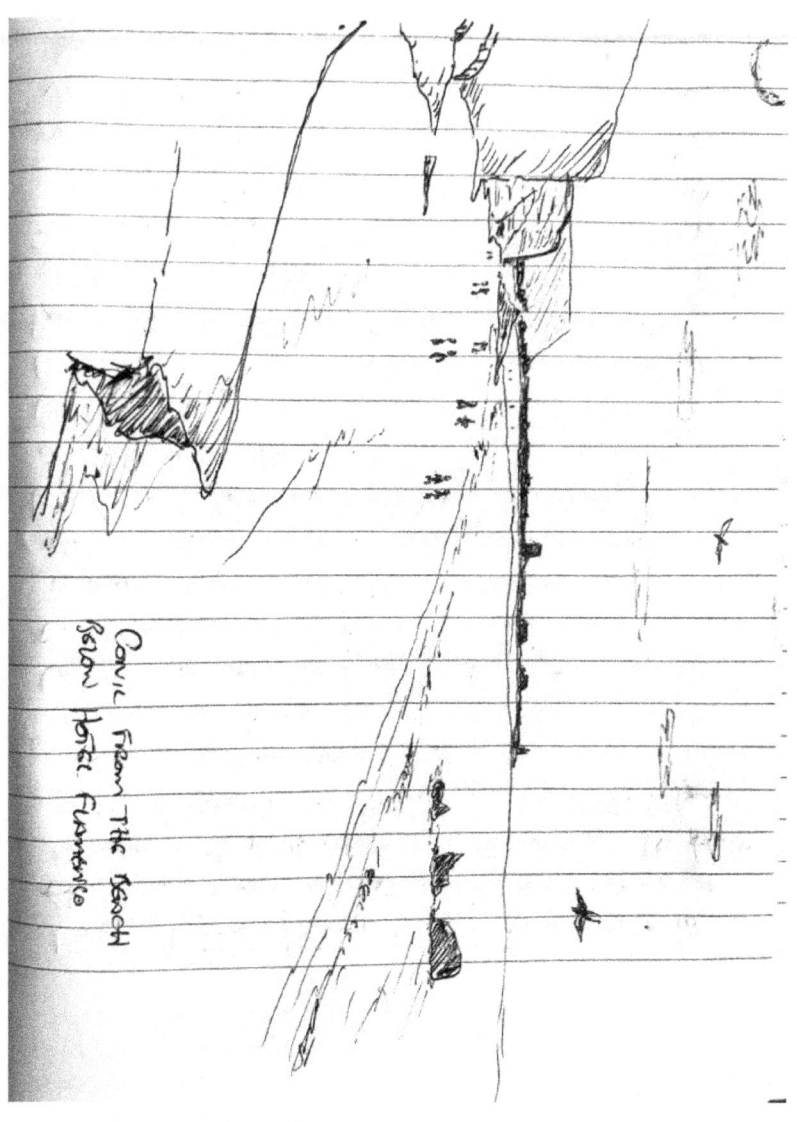

Conil from the beach below Hotel Flamenco

El Palmar

Well today turned out to be most interesting. I got a map from Conil *Touristica* and headed to the edge of town. From there I could see El Palmar, maybe 3km away. I was at the road leading out of town and had to decide whether to hitch-hike or make the beach walk. Using my new found sense of decision making, I opted for the beach, and a wise move it later turned out to be. I made El Palmar within 40 minutes of hip-swing walking even against some pretty heavy winds.

I later took the road route by car, and it is a pig of a journey. 10km at least, I reckon. Though its one redeeming feature is the ranch brothel that stands out like a Wild-West saloon and goes under the cover of being a large and grandiose Hotel. Apparently the 'clubs' here aren't clubs at all but are bordellos, and most exist outside of the towns. I guess everyone likes it that way for their own particular reasons.

The stretch of beach between Conil and El Palmar was amazing. Dead land behind it renders it empty and only accessible from either end, and as I walk in the desert-like conditions, I realise that I have never been so alone on such a large beach before. Two dots in the distance soon become a couple walking. The wind blasts me mercilessly, but I push on. My hip-walk is in flow, learnt from watching the athletes compete in the Commonwealth games. I assume it must be the most efficient form of high-speed walking and seems to work well. I make El Palmar and step off the beach onto a single track road. It is dead. A ghost town. The waves are low and clouds once again cover the sun.

Wandering the deserted beach road, I begin to wonder what on earth I came here for. There are some houses for rent. All appear to be empty. There is no life here at all. Not a soul. I walk maybe another kilometre deciding that since I have come this far, I may as well do the entire length of the place. I felt certain I was drawn here, maybe all will be revealed. I walk for a while longer and then turn a corner and see

El Palmar

Bar So-Co. I wander up. It is an open-fronted place, almost a wooden shack. I walk in.

All three people in the place are English. It is just opening up as I arrive. A bar that opens in the morning is the kind of bar that I like. There is a good stock of booze on the shelves along the back wall and some tables out front with further stools along the front of the bar. The place is run by Patrick, a Brum (Birmingham) originally, but moved out to Spain from Devon. He has rented the bar with his sister, who is also in there. Another woman, Anne, works in the bar and she turns out to come from Northolt of all the places, it is only a mile from where I live! It's all a bit surreal. I am overjoyed to find my first English people and better still, ones I can relate to. I feel like I have arrived. I am very emotional. The Coronas, that I excitedly down, kick my ass pretty quickly as I was nearly dead from all the walking. The conversation lifts and drops in waves. The bar has the feel of a place that comes alive slowly but stays open as long a someone is in there willing to buy a drink.

It turns out that Patrick has had the place for just two months, though he has been out here since last year, and tells me that this whole area goes bonkers with Spanish in the summer. I like El Palmar, and Patrick offers to take me back to Conil to get my stuff. This takes three more beers and various bizarre Spaniards arriving before it gets even close to happening, and then the actual owner, Hector, shows up. Sometime after that, we are able to leave. I am just glad not to have to make the walk again. I have only seen the north corner of El Palmar, and as I head out with Patrick it dawns on me that I may have burned my bridges by drunkenly agreeing to things so readily. My head swoons, and I am now wrapped up in having to make small-talk, but he is easy going and I am still blown away by the find. He gives me the local story as we drive, and explains his place in it. I hear about the Levante wind that currently batters us, and will slowly turn into raw heat. The girl from Northolt has a kid out there, and her husband rents surf kit. I had already met him, he reminded me of Dale Dagger, the trusty mariner and ex-surfer who showed me around San Juan Del Sur in Nicaragua. Similar kind of a guy. It's clearly not yet the main season in El Palmar, but I am blown away by the open generosity and kindness from all of them, things seem to be falling nicely into place. I knew I had to go to El Palmar. I cash out of the tent-site at Conil and pack up my stuff, throwing it into Patrick's car and then we head back.

We come back via El Palmar's official campsite, which turns out to be closed. Patrick says he has a spare bed, for which I am suddenly very grateful. Still feeling the beers from earlier, though they are wearing off a bit, we roll back into the bar and I immediately order up another one. I also order some small tapas. I dump my essentials in his spare room, which is a small affair just around the back of the bar-shack-cum-home. He sleeps somewhere a little further round from that. I then take a walk to the beach to check out the waves, catch some sun that is finally now breaking out, and to look for the second campsite that I know exists someplace. It has been great to bump into people and fun too, but curiously I already miss the solitude. No offence to them, but meeting new people was never my strong point when it comes to sustaining the conversation. Even so, it has given me a place to put my head for the night and to enjoy the company as it comes by.

7 pm finds me still wandering, and I meet Hector again, who catches me writing at another bar that is a bit quieter. I feel as if I miss Conil in some strange way. I guess I just don't want the bother of my own knee-jerk reaction to meeting strangers and having to now socialise. It's nice, but it catches me out; how I now feel obligated at some level. All I end up doing is getting drunk and gibbering inanities, and I can do that at home in London. Still, I find no other campsite, so tonight I am in the kind hands of So-Co, which took me a while to realise it stands for south coast, though this is the west coast in my mind, I think it is actually more south-west, but whatever.

Now, the beer has worn off, and I feel a lot less fun than I did earlier, so I duck into a place called El Torre to eat. I am the only person in there. The weirdest and ugliest food on earth is served up to me, but I need to eat something and this is about my only option in El Palmar without going back to So-Co. I try a bit and it tastes okay, though I fear the end result. I also discover mosquito bites. I knew it was all going too well.

El Palmar

Hector told me that I can camp in the bushes by the beach this time of year, but I don't fancy that idea. Stray dogs and people pissing after leaving So-Co isn't my preferred zone of sleep. El Palmar is a perfect spot though, everything about it is cool, a nice, long stretch of sand with one road along it. It is empty, calm, flat land. No hotels, no high-rises, no buildings showing signs of tourism at all. Lazy looking cafes are dotted along it's mile long shoreline and most barely seem open, but having no campsite here for me to tent at, that is a pain.

I'll stay at So-Co tonight, but I need to pitch my tent rather than stay in rooms. It's what I want, it is what I came out here for. The natural, relaxed situation, in the open air. And I actually want it to be solitary. I had not realised this aspect until now. A slight twinge in my stomach now, a hint of anxiety coming back again, my earlier sense of joy has waned. I best return to So-Co soon, if only out of politeness, and to check that Pat is still cool with me staying. It's quiet everywhere else in El Palmar anyway. Don't know what I'll do for chat from this point on, I have kind of run out of stuff to say. Probably ought to get the guitar out, though I have little doubt that it will annoy anyone in there. I don't fancy doing that right now anyway. Waves look like they are picking up a bit. Seen a surfer out there trying hard, but not much happening for him. Not enough to do anything on yet. Got sand in my ass too, goddamn it, I hate that. Hangover hitting hard on me now. Yikes. Always the way. When I am in unfamiliar surrounds, I drink to get through the discomfort, though at least I stop before I get sick these days.

I roll back into the bar feeling tired and a bit bemused and sit front-and-centre on a bar stool. I can barely talk. Pat is on his bar shift now and has Julio helping him. Julio is wiry and jumpy, but a friendly young character with a cheeky grin and the look of Mister Bean. The only other person sat at the bar with me is the once animated Juan Manuelo, who now swoons face down asleep with his forehead on the bar. Pat tells me that he just ordered four beers for himself, but passed out on the first. They are lined up in front of him. He is, apparently, Pat's plumber. He came to fix a leaky toilet and took the whole day to do the job - in true Spanish style - because he was stopping every ten minutes for a beer. That was two days ago. He has been in the bar

The Road to El Palmar

spending what he earned for the job ever since. Spaniards. I like them. Hector is in again, turns out he rents the place to Pat for 600 euros a month. A good deal in high season, I expect. I still can't talk much, but the post-Corona pain is easing, and thankfully that curious dinner hasn't struck me down yet. Hector leaves to go to a fiesta with the local 'talent', which someone then observes was mutton dressed as lamb. At least I wont be chasing women the next few days, that much is clear, and actually comes as a relief. I am trying to outgrow those old ways, now that I am reaching a respectable age, lest I become just an aged pervert. I mean it is wrong, isn't it? Or is it.

I give in finally to the pain, and order a whisky and coke. You don't get measures in south-west Spain they just pour it in liberally, as it should be done. Moments later I feel as right as rain again, and though I still can't talk, I see that twilight is descending on my happy pain and the orange and red glow lights up the glass behind the bar, throwing out colours all around. I begin to warm back up to life. This feeling reminds me of just how amazing it is to be here in this curious place right now. It's like I made it to where I was supposed to be. The strangest and least known bar, somewhere at the edge of the world, out in the middle of nowhere, in a corner of a little known place called El Palmar, yet still so alive in its own way. It feels somehow very strange to be here. I swing between comfort and discomfort. So, I drink to cover up the discomfort, and that works well enough for now. I guess it's actually a problem most of us have, we don't really know what to say to each other. That should be fine, to just sit and say nothing, but it isn't. It makes it really quite awkward and uncomfortable a lot of the time. The four of us hang there in the bar. The silence in me reaching a bursting point as I struggle for places to look, and things to look at, that I haven't looked at already. I just have nothing to say. It's diabolical that at aged nearly 40, after all the things I have seen and done, that I still cant hold a conversation with strangers for very long. It seems even stranger that I cannot do it in some far-flung land, and in a place that I will probably never be again. This issue vexes me.

Then it dawns on me that maybe talking simply isn't what I do, so maybe I should just do what I do instead. Aided in this slightly suspect scheme by the next whisky and coke, I sink it quickly and then rise

El Palmar

from the stool to go to collect my beloved travel companion, Jacqueline, my acoustic guitar. Returning to my seat with her, I feel a mix of bashful stupidity and impending expectation as Pat and Julio eye me suspiciously. I know what they are thinking, because I think the same when people appear with guitars in my vicinity. I catch their glance to one another, but this is something I have to do. I am unapologetic because I know this is important for me, and I have been failing to do what I need to do thus far. This is where I will make my debut. El Palmar, So-Co. Tonight. I have decided.

I start to twang along gently to the Café Del Mar music that is playing. Julio stops the music demanding a song, but I ask him to put it back on, and just let me play along for a while to warm up. I quietly curse myself for letting my once finely-tuned ability to jam along to anything, fade this last decade. I hit bum notes and feel cack-handed, so I order up another whisky and find the medicine is slowly taking me where I want to be. The guitar; my love, my story, and to some extent my regret. The one thing that has been with me all these years, waiting there like a faithful companion, though in the end doomed to become neglected. I start to warm the finger muscles and relax into that familiar feeling.

I am now in a place where I don't have to talk any more, the anxiety is dispelled, and my fingers doodle up and down the fret-board. I disappear into it. This is my home, this is where my energy finds expression, it is where I find my place in the world and where the world makes sense to me. Everything becomes forgotten when I immerse myself in music, and I like that. This is my only form of communication that does not make me anxious in expressing it, though I am still terrified of the reaction when I do. The tune on the stereo comes to an end and there in that bar with two barmen and a passed-out Spaniard, I finally surface above the waters that I have been lost in for nearly a decade. I begin to sing and play.

I will remember this night, and I know it. It marked itself upon me and in a good way. Somehow I came here to do this thing. The calling I felt, to be at this spot and this moment in time, a little town on the south-west of Spain called El Palmar. It sounds so cliched and yet it is true. The place where some kind of re-birthing happened, a reminder of who I once was, of who I wanted to become, but failed. The part of me resurfaced that I had let go of ten years previous when the decision was finally made to join the rat-race. A musician is what I never became, but wanted to, and I guess some dreams just never come to be, and we have to accept that somehow.

Most of my favourite songs are laments, I like the tone of grief in a song, something that touches you in the heart and makes you feel and let out a sigh. I prefer that kind of song to the more raucous stuff, when armed with an acoustic guitar, at least.

As I played, a couple came into the bar, and when I stopped they urged me to play some more. Suddenly I had a small audience that seemed appreciative, and that felt damn good because I don't really think Pat was with me on it at all. The new guy hummed along, knowing the tune, his eyes sparkling with pleasure that then fed me, giving me the confidence I so long craved to feel again. I played a couple more tunes, and then put the guitar down. You can definitely over-do these things.

For the rest of the night I'd talk for a while, then pick it up, and strum along unobtrusively to whatever was playing. Juan the Spanish plumber woke up during my initial rendition and then came and sat closer to me. He reminded me of a crazy little monkey. All sparkling eyes, wild hair, and lively, humorous conversation that I barely understood a word of. He then introduced me to the music of Paco de Lucio, getting Julio to put it on the sound system. I could not believe the skill I was hearing. Juan loves his music, and clearly knows the best. He explained Paco to me, his skill, his art, his passion. I felt humbled in a good way. It was giving me aspiration, I realised how much the flamenco style of playing appeals to my intuitive, natural way much more than, say, classically learnt guitar. To be a good *flamenco* guitarist you have to play with your heart, to be a good *classical* guitarist you have to play all the right notes. This was my education that night, and I understood what I had found and had been missing all this time. It is why I never learnt to read music, I had refused to learn, because I did not want to have an imprint put upon the music that I felt came out of me quite naturally. Until then I had no real idea why I had resisted that, I just thought I was too lazy to learn the structures. But it was actually

El Palmar

because, for me, the classical way completely lacked passion and could kill the music in you. I could not engage it, and it did not engage me to want to learn to read music that way, so I had stopped learning it.

I recognised some of Paco de Lucio's licks and style from Balearic clubbing tracks and Cafe Del Mar chill-out too, but I had never known who he was until that night. Juan enlightened me. He knew a lot about him. He understood his playing style. My childish twang was no match for a flamenco master like Paco, he cut the air with runs and chords I could only dream of. That night was giving me a taste of something I could never hope to attain, and yet was giving me understanding of what a complete devotion to the guitar, mixed with a natural born talent, could become. He was the best, not just one of them, but *the* best, a true maestro. I twanged along, enjoying trying to follow parts even in a small way towards where he went with them. It was hopeless, of course. Every now and then Juan would grab my shoulder, or put his hand on my strings to stop me, and he'd bid me to follow him as he shut his eyes and let his heart follow the tune that Paco then played. I felt each moment being pulled out of my heart, undeniably magical sounds taking us away in what felt like the epitome of guitar perfection. I literally could have cried at moments when I realised where I was, and how I got to be there that night. It seems silly to read it now, but I know it hit me that deeply to be there.

It was 1 am when I finally paid my bar-tab, and then I wandered round the corner to my room and fell drunkenly to sleep. No one else had come into the bar that night. I fell into intoxicated slumber. I knew that I had made it to the place that I was meant to be. I had crossed some threshold in my life that night too, though I did not know it then, nor quite what it would mean for me.

This is the end

I woke before dawn and felt a familiar fear awake in me also. That good old irrational fear of death. That question we can't face, nor quite figure out, yet can't avoid either in the end. The shape of the dawn light coming through the bars of the window made it look like a crucifix was hanging up there, and that was when I thought that I have come here to die. Drawn like a moth to the flame. I feel an inescapable fear. *Just try to relax, you stupid bastard!*

Pat telling me last night how the great white shark comes here to breed. Maybe he was pulling my leg, I don't know, but I sensed that powerful tug in me that recognises my end. Sharks certainly capable of conjuring it. The price I pay for over-sensitivity, maybe, or for opening those doors of perception that I shouldn't have all those years ago. Or maybe everyone gets this, but just never mentions it for fear of being judged emotionally weak and a little too morbid.

I try to find the strength to accept that this fear on me may not necessarily mean bad things. Just because I felt like something drew me here to El Palmar, it could mean good things too. But why is it such a terrifying and debilitating sensation that keeps creeping up on me? Why is death so obsessively, morbidly, of concern to me at the moment? Why is it so hard to accept, that one day it really will be our last day on earth? Why do we never talk to each other about death? We only ever run and hide from it. Yet, it is our death that draws us on through life.

I find myself wondering about that now, as I watch the dawn light grow gently stronger, and the cross of my damnation throws it's shadow down onto the bed. How will I face mine? Will I be strong enough to laugh at it as it strikes me down? I don't have the answer, or unfortunately maybe I do. I will probably cower before it and beg death to leave me alone, go pick on someone else. And yet how important this question has always been, as much as we ignore it constantly. Death. The ultimate question without answer. It lies at the

This is the end

bottom of all my longings, and it fuels the reason for my searching, endlessly, fruitlessly. The root of every answer I have been looking for all along, is probably death. The end. The completion. Life closing the circle. What if, all this time, I have been looking for the end? What a goddamn waste that would be. I lay waiting to know more, and at some point during my churning, percolating anxiety attack, I fell back to sleep.

I awake again a little later feeling differently, the death obsession is mostly gone. I feel more at home again, comfortable, as if I have arrived at a destination that I have been heading towards for years. It is not El Palmar itself, nor the people, nor the bar, nor the beach, nor in the ascetics of the place, so much as in the feeling I have found by being here. There is all the discomfort associated to being around strange people, but beyond that, beneath it, is this other feeling. It is one of freedom, anonymity, distance from the world that I have become so familiar with. It feels like I am in a place between worlds, in the mist, briefly lost in time. I have found something here. Maybe just because I made it to here. I travelled following a calling in order to find it, and it just happens to be right here. It took a certain amount of sacrifice, risk, action following invisible things and climbing over obstacles to achieve it. Not least the guilt of abandoning my friends when they wanted me to be around. Leaving my girlfriend behind when she wanted to come. Giving up *this* and sacrificing *that*. All for selfish reasons just so that I could get to be here, where I am right now, in space and time. In this particular moment. I feel momentarily complete, yet also terrified because of what it may mean. The fear of the unknown basically translating into a fear of death, and I think that is what keeps manifesting in me, and why I keep banging on about it in this journal. I am afraid, but also excited by what I am finding.

As I fall back into sleep once more, I realise that I have no choice but to make peace with my world, and my life, and my death too. I need to do all this, while I still have time. Maybe it is right to say our farewells and our thank-you's sometimes, just in case it is our last day. There is some sense in doing that. Make peace with our lives, where-ever we wake up in them, even if unexpectedly and for just a brief moment. Wherever we find ourselves thinking about it, and when we do, make peace with it right then and there. Death is always listening, and waiting, and creeping towards us. And when that black-shadow does finally come, whether it is today, or tomorrow, or whenever it happens to be and however grisly it chooses to make our exit, at least let it find us doing the things that we love. I am not sure we have power over any other choice, but that one. The Desiderata is right - we do owe it to ourselves to strive to be happy, and this was my attempt.

The way of the guitar

Well I am not dead yet! But that hasn't made things any easier either. I get up and go around to the bar to find Pat and Anne awake and stocking up. I order breakfast, and once again take my same position on a stool at the bar and not long after a few morning pleasantries, fall quickly into silence. I really have nothing much to say. Finishing breakfast, I go back to my room to wash and shave only to discover my shampoo bottle has exploded in my rucksack. It's worse than water, and as I try to wash it out everything is now getting very frothy. Never put shampoo in the main section of a rucksack, it takes a good hour to sort out.

As I finish up, a girl I haven't seen before comes out the back and tells me Nick, the surfer guy, is here. I follow through to the bar and meet Nick, a well-dressed, blond haired, thirty-something. He is the local surf-school teacher, but he doesn't look like your traditional surfer at all. He is friendly, English, and within minutes of talking has invited me to Portugal on a surf run at the end of the week with his mates. Sounds great! He then hears about my guitar debut the night before and on the spot invites me to come and play at his birthday bash the next night. Even better! I can't wait. This all conveniently decides for me the one question that I had been starting to mull over a bit, whether I should stay. I am now definitely staying in El Palmar.

Nick reckons the waves are building, and that finally now the Levante from the Sahara has stopped we can expect a better swell tomorrow. I had noticed that a lot of people had really very bad hay fever while the Levante blew, and he tells me that it carries bacteria and as a result many people get ill from it. He offers me a surf board and wet-suit for the next two days and lets me have it for the price of one. It's fifty euros, which is pretty pricey for a day, but I feel I am in good hands and since he is the only outlet in the place, there is little choice anyway. I tell him, truthfully, that I really am not much good yet, and he tells me about his near-death experience in an Atlantic wave. Every surfer has their story of the wave that nearly got them, right up until the wave that does.

The thing about the sea that I am acutely aware of, is that even though I am drawn to it and love what I have discovered in surfing, as soon as I step foot into the ocean I cease to be at the top of the food chain. Man is prey out there, for sharks or just the power of the waves. Nature has too much opportunity to get at you on the ocean. I still need guidance out there on a board, and I like a bit of company too. I can get up on a wave and follow it in, but I haven't got the hang of manoeuvring about much, nor overcoming my fear of death by large fish or dark shadow. Anyone willing to be out there with me gives my mind a rational safety-line and also logically reduces my nibble factor by half. There are a few submerged rocks on El Palmar's shoreline too, I spotted them while the tide was out and took a note of where they were.

Nick is also a friend of the character that I met yesterday, and it seems they are all professional-level surfers. It's a golden opportunity for me to learn. I check my monetary situation. I have 200 euro left in cash, maybe I can pay for the trip to Portugal on a bank card. I am on course financially, but won't be able to afford my part of the petrol to Portugal, nor board hire, without getting out more money. It is another good reason to camp beach-side for the next few nights. I don't want to abuse the kindness of Pat, who has put me up in a real bed this last night, and the money saved can then go on the board hire. I'll just have to risk being eaten in my sleep by the bloody great stag beetles that inhabit the grassland dunes out the front of So-Co. After walking the beach, I decided that the best place to remain hidden while also enjoying the ocean view was actually right outside the bar that I was currently habituating. So-Co beach front, in the bushes, on the beach, will be my chosen bed for tonight. It's got enough cover to hide me from the Civil Guardia and has a nice, condo-style view of the beach too. What more could a guy ask for?

It's 2 pm. It's Friday. And I decide to head over to the beach to top up my sunburn. I think that I finally spot a pair of breasts, but the only other people on the beach are too far away for me to be sure.

The way of the guitar

Hang on. Yes. Those are naked breasts. Confirmed sighting. I had almost forgotten that women existed, now that the guitar and me are back on.

I dreamed in the night that I won a writing competition with the Harrow Times. 700 quid. Felt good, almost prophetic somehow. I think I went on to dream about making music too, but that bit is vague now. Why are dreams so hard to remember once you are fully awake? Our dreaming memory is totally separate to our conscious one, and it's not a simple case of trying to recall the events of a dream, it is shrouded from us once we wake. I try to recall it further now, but without success. It's all just a vague, hazy blur, and yet the feeling of it lingers. A uniquely dream-like feeling. That feeling somehow manages to make the light of day, where the memory doesn't.

I would like to understand what changed last night, and what I found here, and why I had to come here, of all places, to find it. I found whatever it was that I was looking for in El Palmar, in this precise moment of time and place. I get a vast fear wash over me when I entertain this thought, as if I am not permitted to ask it, as if some terrible woe awaits me if I dare to try to pull back the curtain on it all. *Just don't ask questions,* some voice in me says. I leave it for now, let it be, for fear of ruining it. Fear is sometimes so superstitiously driven, though, isn't it?

Then the memory of Juan and listening to Paco de Lucia comes back to me, and I smile. The masterful ability of the likes of guitarists such as Paco also begs the question - *who taught the first flamenco player his art?* Where does it all arise from? His skill is so far above the other guitar players of the world, that it is an almost divine power that has been granted the true flamenco marksman - the ability to grasp the passion of the heart and express it almost violently through their fingertips. And yet it is so much more than just the movement of the fingers, it is the passion itself. And the whole body engages in it, not just the hands. Juan told me that Paco once broke his foot and as a result could not play, he needed his whole body movement to be able to engage his art properly.

So, I got a glimpse of that pathway to passion through the guitar and with Juan's help last night. The entrance that leads to that place.

The Road to El Palmar

Juan was trying to explain aspects of it. The religion of it, almost. How a man must walk alone with just his guitar, must completely embrace it, love it, become it. Someone told me once that Jimi Hendrix slept with his guitar. You hear a lot of things, but somehow that one made some kind of sense to me, because once I used to do it myself. Mostly that happened because I was playing it so much I would fall asleep while doing so, and every night it was the same for many years. The true art of music in any form really isn't born just from lots of practice, nor maybe even learning it at all. It is something else. It's in *the way* of the guitar. The Tao of it. It is brujo, it is a kind of sorcery, it is about our relationship to the gift. That is at the essence of true power. Maybe understanding *that*, is what I came out here to find for myself. And maybe I found that understanding last night. The road to it. Even if I do not take it on myself, I saw something of where it begins, and what such an art actually is.

I am sat on the beach here alone, on soft yellow sand, and looking out to the sea as I think about these things. The fear rises in me again, as if I am thinking sacrilegious thoughts. The way of the guitar. Giving oneself to it. To totally embrace the music you have to give up everything to follow it, only a very few people can do that. You have to have been born with it in you already. I see that, but I don't know if that means I have it in *me*.

Besides which, I was like that once before already, I lived for the guitar and music, but nothing came of it in the end. That surprised me, and confused me. Once I lost my confidence then I had to give it up, and it took a lot of hard work to let it go but in my confusion, I was getting ill. Not eating, not doing anything else but playing the guitar and waiting for the gods to notice. I wonder if I got something wrong in my choices, or maybe I panicked and gave it all up too soon. It is hard to know. There were a lot of good reasons for letting the music dream go and heading towards a career path instead. It was hardly an easy choice, it was pretty much my only one at the time. I was 27 before it finally became too much to continue, how much longer could I have gone on in the way that I was? Not much longer. But what did I lose out on by making that decision to let the guitar and music go?

Maybe I am just too lazy and easily distracted to become as good

The way of the guitar

as someone like Paco, or maybe now is the moment for me to revisit that question, and to re-consider the way of the guitar. Am I willing to give up everything for that one true love, to sell your soul for that passion. There is a fear in putting it like that. Really it is just about an absolute alignment to a single pathway of devotion and knowledge. Embracing your innate passion in order to become a particular thing. That alignment of one's being with that of the spirit of the guitar. That is what Paco De Lucia clearly achieved. He became the music, completely.

In some ways I feel as if it would be the cure for all my pain and fears. If I was only able to fully embrace it, let go to the music and the guitar again, I might feel that deeper sense of purpose and meaning that has become lost to me. But then again, I knew unequivocally who I was back then too, I knew what I was, and there was zero doubt in me at all for many years. I spent my entire youth trying to do just that, become a guitar virtuoso, but I failed, so what gives? I already tried an absolute immersion in it, so how could that be the key that unlocks the door for me? Besides, this romantic ideal is all well and good to entertain while out here, but I wonder if I would be able to maintain it when I returned to the hard, busy world of suburban survival. What would I tell my bills, debts and obligations that await my return to England?

I am going back to the guitar, I don't care about you anymore, I don't need a roof over my head, nor food, nor love thank you very much, I am just fine, it's just me and my guitar from now on. We are back on, and we are going to make it.

These next few days need to cement the decision in me, one way or the other. No, that's the wrong word. I need to *align* myself with this way if I am going to embrace it, familiarise myself with it, submerge and drown myself in it, marinate myself in *the way,* until I am drenched from the top of my head to the bottom of my soul in it. If I do this, then it needs to be so strong and so absolute that nothing in that hot, arid, bleaching desert that is city life as an IT rat, a small cog in the wheels of industry, none of that can any longer be allowed to get through to me and create any semblance of doubt. I have to be willing

The Road to El Palmar

to die for my art. I need to return to my love of the guitar, re-kindle my passion for it, embrace it in such a way that I no longer do anything else and refuse all other distractions.

But even as I write those words in an attempt to sound convincing to myself, the truth is that I am 37 years old, and I just don't know how to keep that fire alight in me any more. It went out over 10 years ago and has been in slow decline ever since. But maybe now is not the time to worry about that, because now is the time to dive into my guitar again, to embrace my re-discovered passion, and if it holds true this time then fantastic, and if it doesn't, then so be it too.

Quite out of the blue, I then recall that my dream was not of me, but of Andre, a musician friend from my place of work. I dreamed that he found success. He is a good musician and works hard at it too, if anyone deserves it, he certainly does.

It is now 3 pm. I am on the beach, enjoying the first proper sunbathing session since I got here. But I think I need to find some shade, and I need to find my guitar.

Camped on beach in covered bushes at El Palmar just above the sands

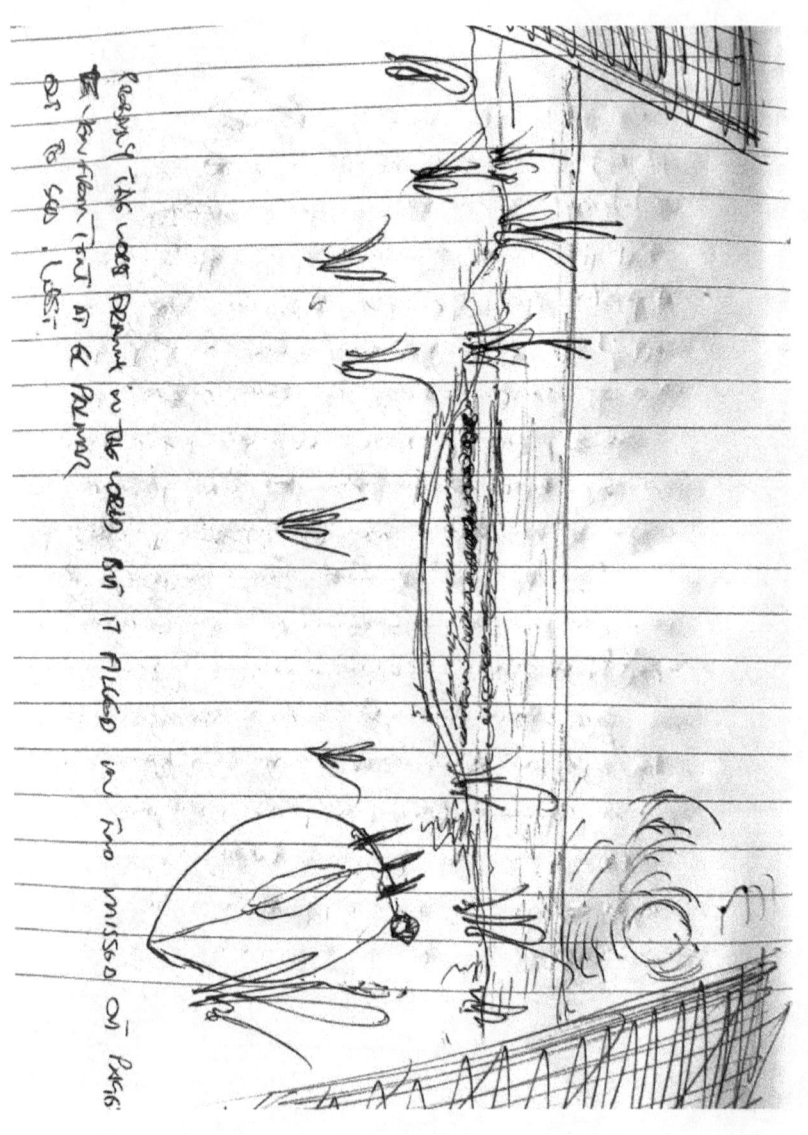

View from tent at El Palmar out to sea. West

The Battle of Trafalgar

The beach is busier this afternoon, I guess people are starting to take their weekend holidays now that the wind has dropped. I am camped up on the beach in the place that I mentioned, almost opposite So-Co bar. Bought some food from the super market, but it is too hot to eat in the tent, as it isn't well shaded. I may regret the tent positioning at sun up tomorrow, but I did not want to stick it right underneath one of those bushes, so I pitched it between a bunch of them and that gives me a nice protection against being seen from the road.

Late afternoon is drawing near, and I feel a low hum of melancholy. I don't want for company though, I am enjoying the solitude now I have found it again. A lone sail boat drifts quietly by on the horizon and I watch it. A memory comes to me, of high summer and my first year in London, with new found friends and my dreams of rock stardom fresh, alive and everything was ahead of me. It was a good year. I had an incorrigible belief that all would turn out exactly as I planned it. There was so much to do in the music scene that surrounded The Marquee Club in those days on the Charing Cross Road where I seemed to land. The heady heights of the early nineties, when everyone was buzzing with a sense of freedom and fun.

The spinning of the wheels of life. Times come and they go, scenes change like merry-go-rounds, you jump on and are either eventually thrown off, or they slow to a halt and you move on. Nothing lasts forever, yet each moment holds an eternity in its own way if you could only recall it all later. That is the hard bit, most of the time I really can't, and that loss seems such a waste to me too. But I guess these are all the moments and feelings that I should be putting into my guitar, rather than just sitting here thinking about it all nostalgically. But the heat is only just bearable out here, and I find it easier to write instead.

I don't think the excess damaged us back then as much as we were

The Road to El Palmar

told that it would. The pills and acid haze was just part of the whole experience, and it did no more damage in the long run, than life itself was capable of doing to us anyway. A lot of people will never be the same again, sure, and some never made it through at all, but mostly it seemed that it was only because they never figured out how to turn around and aim for higher ground when the time called for it. I was one of the casualties on a couple of occasions, you pick yourself up, you get on.

The last two years have also been giving me warning signs. If you crash once and survive, then you should probably make sure you do not make the same mistakes again. The warning signs are always there, if you care to look. I probably wont completely stop taking drugs, but the roads we travel on are the roads that shape us, and I don't really want to find myself in bad shape in ten years time because of my choices now.

As you get older, suddenly the future starts to matter, and that comes attached with a fear. There was a time when all that seemed important was to be able to do drugs until the dawn-light. Nowadays I want my mind and my health to remain in one piece. Somehow that becomes more important, and I guess that is where the fear of death starts to creep in.

There is only really one thing I would change if I could because there is not much I regret at all, and that one thing I would change is - *how to have a normal conversation with people that I don't know*. It seems to me that it should be a lot easier than it is. Instead I find there is a constant influx of all-absorbing, overwhelming information going on. My brain seems to stop being able to think clearly when in the company of strangers. It's annoying as much as it is overwhelming and often throws me into silence. That is also the problem with drink and drugs, because they help me over that hurdle. That makes them dangerous, and I started to realise that was why I was using them so much. I was using them in order to be around people, and pretty soon I did not know how to be around people without them. And just as this trip is now proving to me, I clearly still don't.

Then a year or two ago, I figured that meditation might be the thing that I needed to take on in order to replace the gaping-hole that

The Battle of Trafalgar

would be left behind if I stopped using drink and drugs. I realised then, that I have a fear of missing out. Maybe on the inner adventure and the spirit of joy and abandon that I find in those ways. It is fun after all, at least until it isn't.

Meditation is a long road to travel and a very slow one too. But every step of the meditation journey gives you something wholesome, whereas drink and drugs mostly just take anything wholesome away. Useful as they may be for shifting gear on your mood or getting your tongue loose, they are not a good answer to anything at all and only ever lead to a bad place in the end. Drink and drugs used to be fun, something changes along the way, and then pretty soon they start to take you to hell. This is true. And sure, the joy of meditation is probably a real thing once you learn it, but it is clear that it has to be earned over the course of many years to make even small bits of progress, while the joy of substance intoxication is super fast, like a fleeting mirage, and it's a short-cut. Worse, they are an avoidance. I certainly use them now to avoid what I probably should be facing up to.

Its going to be a long, hard journey to give it all up completely, and I am not even sure I will succeed. The anxiety I feel a lot of the time is an utter bastard. I don't really know how you give it all up successfully, you can't just stop, you have to find the correct replacements and then slowly wean yourself off the drugs and onto those things instead. I am not even talking about heroin nor any of the officially addictive drugs. I am talking about all the others that are supposedly not addictive, you still get addicted to an aspect of them that provides a crutch, and that is the truth. Even so, I would not give up my years spent using them either, because I had a lot of fun. But I know it is time to be getting away from all forms of drink and drug intoxication. That is now my plan. I know that I drink a lot still, and it has increased while out here. But going into some sort of denial and shut-down would be even more of a mistake. I also know that the drinking is a large part of why I get the late night anxiety attacks, but then if I don't drink, I still get them anyway. I have a lot to look at.

Giving anything up is hard. It leaves a vacuum behind and that sucks other things in. Nature abhors a vacuum, I think I said that

The Road to El Palmar

already. There is a proper way to give things up, and I have not yet figured it out, but I will. There is clearly a right way and a wrong way. I have tried to stop various vices by just dropping them but soon find myself failing. Failing is always hard to take. Same thing with smoking, it's all about addictions, and I haven't figured out how to stop that yet either.

I have stopped womanising though, which is a surprising relief, at least for this holiday. Though maybe it would have made for better reading, or more likely not. It is such a pointlessly addictive conquest, like dogs chasing rabbits round a track. The attraction is still there, sure, but it's such a waste of time and energy chasing women. I am also told it is somewhat disrespectful of women's finer qualities, but I find that a little bit suspect, women like sex as much as we do, so what is that baloney all about? Still, the interest for me never really was in the woman, but something else, maybe the light that draws me in. Then one day I realised what it was that I was chasing. It dawned on me that sex relieves the anxiety I feel, just like getting high does. So sex was a cure for anxiety too, for me at least. So mostly all these things come down to a question of why that anxiety is there in the first place, and what to do about that. I don't have any answers yet.

I ate in the late afternoon at So-Co again. I spent dinner chatting to Gary, the husband of Anne, and it turns out he is also from Northolt, though he hasn't been back there since the '70s. After eating we continue chatting and knock back eight of the local Gruzcampo lagers that go down way too easily, but it is the cheapest drink in the bar at one euro a pop. The sun is setting by the time we are done, and it explodes again onto the mirrors behind the bar, bouncing back through some yellow spirit bottles. It mesmerises me into a day-dream, and I feel the whole Spanish vibe light up in me once more. Julio has promised to cut me a CD of Paco, who plays again now in the bar, setting the mood beautifully. Then Gary tells me about how the Battle of Trafalgar actually went down right off the coast from where we are. He tells me that on the naval charts of the day, it only names the nearest lighthouse and that was the way they used to record naval positions in their logs. Really it all drifted from Trafalgar in the south,

The Battle of Trafalgar

up this way, and the battle went down, right out there. This blows my mind. So, El Palmar was actually the true site of the Battle of Trafalgar, where Nelson died and the long war for control of the oceans by the British Empire was finally won against the Spanish. This little piece of knowledge is huge to me. That battle literally defined the future of Empires, and it happened right here. The carnage of which would have been washing up on the beach where I am now camped.

I thank Gary for the chat, and then take my leave not long after to walk and consider this new piece of information. It makes the whole reason for coming to El Palmar take on a completely new depth of meaning for me. I have always been fascinated by Nelson. My family had a flat up on the citadel in Calvi, Corsica. Calvi is the place he was trying to take when he lost his eye fighting the citadel battlements.

I walk down towards the other bar that is along the beach, the one I had found previously. It is owned by a Spaniard called Carlos. It also has a younger clientele. They are a bit immature and squeaky tonight, and I think I detect a hint of malice from some of them when I enter. Maybe just youthful bravado. I don't know how the Spaniards do it, but if this was Watford I'd have a fight on based on the way they are being. As it is, I am foreign, and so I can pretend to ignore it. I have wandered in with my guitar, inspired by the reaction to last night's performance and today's musings. I am intrigued to see if I am able to spark up in another venue, and if I will get away with it. There are not many people in here, just some of the young locals playing pool, the music is too loud and overly funky for playing along to, so I drink and I write instead. All the while completely ignoring the youth that eye me from the corner. Other than them, it's pretty nice in here, though clearly it's a hang out for the local wannabe-gangster contingent.

Gary also told me that El Palmar beach is now the common venue for high-speed boat landings carrying hash or immigrants from Africa, and as such the place is in fact under high military observation. He reels off a few gunship and chopper incidents to add a bit of authenticity, but I believe. Shit happens. He told me that if I see kids with too much money, then chances are they are on some hash for cash take, and this bar strikes me as a den housing exactly that ilk.

The bar girl is cute, but she also has a bit of attitude, though come

The Road to El Palmar

to think of it she might be Carlos's missus. I didn't know what to make of Carlos. He is in his 30's, has quite chiselled features with dark, tanned skin and black hair, and amazing blue eyes that cut right into you. This has made him a little too vain, and a bit too special to be genuinely friendly. I never understand that offish-ness in people. He is friendly and interested to talk to at first, but then appears disinterested as soon as you start speaking, and you get the feeling that actually he isn't interested at all, he just wanted to hypnotise you with his amazing blue eyes, and when it didn't work, he got bored. Something like that, anyway. And another question I have - why are so many Spanish men so short? Reminds me of the Corsicans. Must be a similar blood line. Mediterranean, or originating from Gaul, or something.

On another note, Pat and Juan said they were up until 5 am last night. I must have bailed four hours before they did. Spain parties on much later than I am used to these days, another way in which I feel old.

I continue to write, planted firmly now at a small table-for-one beside the pool tables. Writing is still a new sport to me, and I have discovered it is a great way to hang out in a place while successfully avoiding threatening eye contact. I can pass the time in my own world, yet remain surrounded by people. Keeping busy with the writing keeps my spirits up, while all the while watching what goes on out the corner of my eye. It's actually quite fun. Writing is good for people-watching, but it also makes those people suspicious I think. Though it may be that the ones in here have something to be suspicious about, if what Gary said is true.

There is an open door in front of me, it faces out of the bar, onto the road and to the beach beyond. There is a nice view through it of the clear, blue and darkening western sky. It is just past sunset, and the moon is following the sunset down, it is in crescent, with a big star not far from it that is shining right on me. It's still kind of magical being here.

As I finish up writing for the evening, I am already feeling somewhat drunk again. I look up to find the entire bar has changed, not a single person is the same, and yet there is the same number of people doing exactly the same things. A strange switch has occurred

The Battle of Trafalgar

while I was lost in the writing. I will set off now, to hit Pat's bar for a few more of his weird cocktail concoctions, and then to bed, perchance to dream.

Map of battle

More pre-dawn musing

I awake again with the fear and with a hangover too. I can see a tunnel of inevitability before me, the woe is on me again. I hear the sea as it pounds against the sand reminding me of the power that pounds us until we all eventually crack. I have to face it, there is nowhere to run. I lie here distressed, right now I don't have the strength to cope, and yet I have to find it. This obsession in me, increasing now as the reality of what I have foreseen and known all along, begins to become clear. I think we already know our deaths. I have no idea how to approach mine with impunity. I feel like a man walking to his execution. I want to cry at this, I want someone to rescue me, I feel the pressure of unfair fates. It's causing me to break down and fall apart. Right here, right now, I want to just fall apart fully and get it over with. Like those days back at school going up to face the cane or the slipper, that long and painful dread in the endless wait. I have it again now. The greatest wait is against our greatest dread - our final outcome.

The coming sun is nearly lighting up the dark sky. Dawn light hints of it's arrival against the effervescent blue walls of my small tent. The new day is nearly here. The sea waves just keep on pounding rhythmically, not hard, but harder than they have been, and it's loud here on the beach. Their sound, a cruel insistence.

What do I do with this truth? How do I put it to rest or make the best of my situation? I do keep getting caught up in these early morning emotional panic attacks. It's obviously not helped by the alcohol. What if last night was my last sunset, and this morning my last hangover? Then these words will be my eulogy. If this is the end, then I never did make it to where I wanted to be, though I think that I lived a great life. Yes, I think I lived it well enough, that is true at least.

I may drown, that is one way to go I suppose. Eaten by sharks? Jesus, why am I thinking about that? Something out there already has us all marked, but some exits are best not thought about. We can feel it waiting out there for us, I think we always could. It's taboo though. We are constantly told - *don't think about it*. Certainly don't write about it, don't bore everyone with my personal emotional crap. But I don't know how to find the balls to walk towards that end, drawn by it, the increasing sound building to a crescendo that becomes the cymbal smash of our inevitability. I let some anger rise, it's my only defence against whatever madness it is that I feel right now, and I am desperately trying to exorcise my way out of it all with this pen. It works a little bit, I suppose.

Oh man! I am more sun-burnt than before and the new day's roaring Spanish sun is nearly up. The heat is increasing in this little A-frame tent of mine, down here on the beach at El Palmar. I best prepare for whatever it brings. They say to overcome your fears you have to face them, but I do not know, nor understand, how you are supposed to face death itself. I guess you just get on with doing what you do, and pretend it is not coming for you, even if the very things you do seem to beckon it.

A thought dawns on me - *maybe my mistake up until now has been to put my focus on the act of death itself, rather than beyond it.* So, I think about what lies beyond that relatively brief but terrifying transitional moment. Doing so, I feel a sense of balance replace the inconsolable fear. So that may work. Now it is beyond death that I focus my intent, out and on towards my definitive journey. Eternity. By god, I think that this has helped. Now I feel as if I want to hit death running, and just explode through it at a billion miles an hour. Like a needle darting through the eye of it, and out beyond. Solid as steel. Fast as light. Smash right through it and be gone, away from this circular madness, finally.

I lie around a little longer, drifting in and out of sleep, my anxiety a riot with the hangover playing a pretty brutal counterpoint, and there is only ever one solution for that. The sun is getting too hot now, and it's not even 10 am. So I get up and wander out to face the fury of the day.

I meet Nick, who says he will be returning for me at midday to take me out surfing. I need a crap, but no bars are open, and I can hardly crap in the bushes nor the ocean, but I find myself looking at both with that question. Eventually get a bite to eat and ablutions are found. Belly feels swollen, must be all the alcohol, as I haven't been

More pre-dawn musing

eating much. Sit in the shade. Wait for the pain to go. It's not so much fun today. In fact, right now, this hurts a lot. Have to avoid the sun as much as possible today too, it is already showing signs of being a scorcher. What the hell am I doing? Pleasure without measure but a pain I actually probably can explain, and I have no one to blame but myself. Them's the breaks.

The sea

What a great day yesterday turned out to be. Something in me seemed resolved by the spiel of my melodramatic pre-dawn writing. On later reading it comes across as dire, indulgent, and narcissistic, yet at the time it really does explain my state rather well. Tempted as I am to destroy such chronically chronicled introversion, I actually think it does me good to get it out, and it is clearly a part of my scrawl on this particular journey. So I have chosen to leave it in, let it be what it is, as raw and embarrassing as that may be.

So, I entered the sea with a determined zeal, and I had an absolute ball. The waves were better than they had been until now, but certainly not beasts. As a result it was pretty easy going, unlike my last surf experience over a year ago now when I went alone on a winter trip to Bude in Cornwall. There I had tall and murderous tumblers to contend with. Today it was just a couple of feet of minor swell, but good enough for my level, and I was up and enjoying my next stages of learning. I haven't yet figured out how to manoeuvre down a wave, and I had to keep an eye out for the submerged rocks too. The sand-bar I was on seemed okay, but I soon drifted towards some suspicious shadows. At one point I swear one moved and the fear hit me again. Turned out to be a rock and not a great white shark.

Now the heat has really switched up a notch, and I decide it's enough for one day. Besides, I want to make Nick's barbecue later and be fresh for it. I head back to my tent and catch an hour siesta, gently frying in there before heading over to Pat's bar to meet up with Anna, and then we head off together. Soon after starting our walk down the road a friend of hers pulls up in a truck. It is another surfer dude with long, black hair, and dark sunglasses. He has a nasally, stoned kind of drawl to his voice, his words of hello rolling lazily out. We climb aboard, and I am squished in with Anna on the front seat, as we head into the back of El Palmar.

Down a couple of dirt tracks we go but after only a few minutes

The sea

driving and we are there. Where is there? It is a huge field, surrounded by other fields that contain bungalows. This field does not. It could be an African ghetto. It's dry and dusty, there are cars, vans, and farm equipment dumped about the place. Long, unkempt and wild grass grows hither and thither and there are even some donkeys grazing. This is Gary's land, I am told. There are also various trucks and a large immobile bus, which turns out to be their home. I love it.

They are different to the travellers I knew in England back in the '80s, when the convoy people were taking a hold and living in lay-byes in broken down buses and vans. Days of Stonehenge festival and the dog-on-a-rope crowd, who lived in shoddy vans and sold Lebanese hash, magic mushrooms, and LSD, and mostly drank Special-Brew lager while moaning about the dole money not being enough. The plan was to smash the system. Their demise was finally brought about by what eventually became known as The Battle of the Beanfield. Not quite as dramatic as The Battle of Trafalgar, though it was bloody, and it was Maggie Thatcher's successful attempt at using riot police to beat the hell of out men, women and children that they had trapped in a field in Wiltshire. All of the people living in the buses that had tried to make their way towards Stonehenge free festival that year. It was 1985. It was also a sorry affair to be caught up in, and we all paid a price for our politics, some more than others. The laws continued to change over the next few years to give the British Government and the Police more power to exert pressure against those kinds of people, eventually pushing them into Wales and into heroin too, but that is another story.

These guys out here are a lot different, they have surf and sea in their blood. It is far more up-tempo, friendly, and they are far easier and more pleasant to be around than the convoy-people tended to be. These people, on the other hand, are out for fun but they are constructive and positive with it too.

I meet some of the families and the small community that has chosen El Palmar as a place to make their home. Nick seems to be the head of this little posse, or maybe it is because it is his birthday that he gets to be king elect. Then there is Julian, who is the guy who gave us a lift over in his truck. Brian, an even more surfer kind of guy, with his raggedy blond hair and stoner refrain. Gary comes out of his immobile home after a while, and there are a couple of other women around who are partners to some of the other guys who I don't know, and then a funny chap whose name I can't remember, even though I spend the closing part of the night hanging out with him.

We all drink and eat, and then the guitars come out. Nick leads. Julian pulls out a gigantic Peavey amp from the back of his truck, which is hilariously unexpected given we are in a field and would have a made a great scene for a Spinal Tap movie. Electric amplification was not what I was expecting, but soon it is up and running and they don't hold back. Suddenly the air is throbbing with raucous guitar, bass, and even singing too. Nick is one of the fastest chord learners I have ever met, and I have a twang of shame as I realise he out-classes me on the guitar. His style is more American blues and the Santana vibe. Perfect and more appropriate for this setting. He is good and holds court, bringing the colour and life in. I am impressed. My acoustic no match for the amped up racket going on, but I don't care. I am just happy to be there and be a part of the fun on that gorgeous, bright and star-filled night. I have without doubt fallen in love with El Palmar.

After a while the racket dies down for a bit, the guitars go away and then talk turns to questions. I am asked why I don't sell up and move out there. I had not entertained the idea until that moment, and it made me think for a minute. I had not considered it to be anything more than a few days of an unexpected detour on my way towards Tarifa and the southern tip of Spain. I only ever thought myself a visitor. It made me think then about Nicaragua. I'd had the idea of going there after being inspired by some friends who were also interested. So as a reconnaissance I went alone, to check it out, to see if it was possible to buy some land together and move out there. It quickly became clear to me that with Nicaragua came problems, and the kind of problems that could escalate more rapidly than I felt comfortable with. But El Palmar is not Central America. I love the idea, and tell them so.

They start to tell me about their plans and the costs of getting a place out there. Thirty grand could get me a ten thousand metre plot right here in El Palmar, just like Gary's. The conversation starts to revolve around money and how to get mortgages on land. It is funny

The sea

how often the discussion of freedom seems to end up straight back at contracts, liens, debts and the need for ridiculous amounts of cash in order for freedom to be achieved. It was the same in Nicaragua, everyone was either talking about the land they were planning to buy, or were trying to show you the land they were hoping to sell. It was talk of living free, and yet curiously living free seemed to mean buying into land on a life-long debt. I was not sure that real freedom actually came with ownership at all. But I was happy to listen, as they all talked about the latest situations in land real estate and the politics of El Palmar's coming infrastructure, an infrastructure which was mostly completely lacking at that moment, hence why they thought the place a good investment. No infrastructure meant no agua, no agua meant no hotels...yet.

I hear Nick and Gary are on the point of setting up the towns first surf shop together. This place is exactly what I was looking for in Nicaragua. Fresh. Just starting. I never found it out there, too many problems hiding behind a false veneer. When I came home, I gave up on the idea of finding somewhere truly wild to go live. But El Palmar.... I don't know. It is certainly tempting to start thinking about that again. These people make it so. The non-urbanised emptiness of the town makes it so. The wildness of it all, makes it so. The good-humoured Spaniards I have met around here, make it so. It is exactly the kind of place I was looking for, in theory, and yet... I feel no excitement, no urge to plan, or trick, or blag my way here. I feel a strange quiet, in fact, and that is something that I don't understand right now.

I sip my beer, and listen to everyone talk excitedly of their lives ahead in El Palmar. Why am I not enthralled by this idea? I don't know. Maybe in some ways I am still in a bit of shock at being here at all. I am also still in the midst of whatever movement has finally pulled me loose from the inertia I felt back home. Loose enough to make me take a leap out alone, following my feet and which eventually brought me to be here... in this mad field, with these amazing people, in El Palmar. What am I doing here? I don't actually yet know. But gaining more possessions and mortgages aren't on my mind right now. Freedom is on my mind. *Freedom*. Whatever the hell that means. I don't want to buy a home nor a piece of El Palmar. I realise something, here,

The Road to El Palmar

right now, in the midst of this night, just as everyone stops talking about how to help me move out to El Palmar and we pick up our instruments again to play. What I realise, is that I am actually trying to find something else by coming here. Something more in tune with the universe, something more natural to life, more aligned to living and to an existence embracing the moment. No cash-deal or ownership can give me that. No mortgage or piece of land can give me that. It's an epiphany of sorts, because it reveals a little more of the puzzle that has been my journey so far. It is about making a deal, maybe, but not with any real-estate agents for some land, but rather with the spirit of life for a sense of true freedom.

I turn down Nick's offer of the Portugal surf run when he brings it up again that night. Something has landed for me. A realisation that this place has shown me something more about the journey, the journey that I barely knew I was on until I got here. As the night slows down and comes to an end, I catch a lift with one of the families that are leaving, and we head to Pat's bar for a last drink. Five drinks later on - and more of Pat's weird cocktail mash-ups - and I have found a true pal in *[I still don't know his name and forgot to write it down, which is annoying because he was exactly my kind of person]*. He makes stupid noises, and constant wise-cracks. More nonsense comes out of his mouth than sense. I can hang around that all night. People who are given to making stupid noises, I seem to be able to be around with ease. They just seem to understand the inanity of meaningful conversation, and are okay with a complete lack of sensibility. Stupid noises make a lot more sense than half the conversations that I have ever had to listen to.

I feel a lot more relaxed tonight. These people are so refreshing. And all of them have sacrificed their lives back home to head out to some crazy, empty surf town without any infrastructure. To live hard, but to live well, and to live right by the sea. The sea. There is something about the ocean that makes the difference to these kinds of tales, without the ocean this merry band of outcasts would not be what they are. The bar would not be what it is, the zest would not be here in quite the same way. The sea has something to do with this story, and I

The sea

listen to it roar in the night as it tumbles relentlessly onto the beach. I am inspired again, and tell the man whose name I have forgotten, that I have changed my mind once again. I want in on the surf trip to Portugal if there is still room. He laughs, and then claps me on the back and says he will text Nick tomorrow about that. And on that note, I've had enough, and I leave to my condo.

The tent
at the beach
El Palmar

I awake again at 8 am and into yet another hangover. The sound of the sea lashing the beach is pleasing to wake up to this time. This really has been a glimpse into the kind of life that I always thought I wanted, and it has been exactly the kind of break that I needed and was looking for. All that I have found here still doesn't quite register in me. I don't suppose it will until I leave. It's all happening too fast to fully grasp or look at with any kind of perspective and understanding. I am in it, as it happens, and right now I just want to live it and love it in that way. I feel freer this morning, less pressured, despite the hangover. I feel comfortable again in myself, like I am on the cusp of great adventures. El Palmar, the place I came all this way to find. Luck mixed with fate and trust brought me to it. And a windy walk down a desolate beach that gave no inkling of what I might find at the end of it all. I did what I had to do, and I made it here. I feel almost fearless at last, as if my prize is within reach because I learnt what I have to do to claim it. How I must clamber over the obstacles that hinder me on the road. I have no idea what the after-effect of this holiday will be, nor how it will effect my life when I get back home. Home seems so distant right now, as if I am caught in a dream, another universe altogether. I could be a changed man and on a mission, or it may just all drift off into forgetfulness, like an idea that was nice but passes away, as they so often do. Those holiday bro-mances, so inspiring at the time. Either way, I know one thing is for sure - something happened for me here. I don't know what that means right now, but I know it is true. Maybe it could have happened anywhere, just the act of leaving home and

The Road to El Palmar

travelling away might have caused it. I don't know. I am all alone, camped on a beach that looks out to the very spot that Nelson died and where England sank the Spanish fleet in a moment that changed the course of history forever. Right here, the world changed entirely.

All the good people I have found here, in a scene so welcoming, and every single one of them eager to help me move out here if I decide that is what I want to do. There is something in this experience that is very heart-warming to me. It is so unexpected. Maybe it is what travel is all about when it is done like this.

I finally passed out with the door of my tent open. In the centre of the opening was an incredibly bright star that made me leave it open and lie back and watch it instead of shutting the night-time world out. I marvelled at the shape it made, it was so bright that it created a triangle, with a central dot of light. I watched it for a long while, waiting to fall asleep. I felt content and happy, at peace in its light, as if there was nothing else in the world that mattered in that moment other than to be right there.

The wind

Surf turned out to be no good today, it's a pity, but this gives me more time to write and meditate. Sitting out in the heat for a while to top up my burn, but it is awkward to write as it gets hotter. I've applied freshly purchased P20 suntan lotion this time, after yesterday's pains I did not want to make it worse. I can't reach my back, so will have to make a point to avoid getting more sun on that. Got to decide what to do after today. Do I leave and continue on my journey south, or stay and risk another night on the beach? I am in two minds about the Portugal run now that I have sobered up, mainly because I can't take my stuff, and it's a six hour drive each way. Not to mention, if I have too much fun, I may never want to come back. With the bus strike on, I can't risk missing the journey back to my old life, appealing as that idea is right now. If the boys can't take me and my gear as well, then I really cant go.

Oddly, I feel I am actually ready to leave El Palmar now. It's like I found what I came here for. I'll sit the day out on the beach and hope for more waves, but it doesn't look likely. Later I'll go check in with Nick, maybe this afternoon, and see if they have enough room for my kit. If I can't go with them, I need to plan what lies ahead. I could stay here again tonight and get drunk in Pat's bar, again, but my mind is wondering if maybe I should move on. Maybe. It's Sunday, and if I stay tonight then I have just tomorrow, and tomorrow night, before I need to hit Conil early on Tuesday to get that bus to Jerez for Wednesday.

I kind of hope I can do the Portugal run so that I am going forward and not retracing my steps, but it could go either way. I have to give the surfboard back tonight anyway, so today is my last chance for any surf here. I don't mind no further surfing action, what I got was good. I need to be ready for the winds to return too. Word is that they may do so tonight or tomorrow, and once they hit, it will be a lot less fun camping on the beach. That Levante will last three days to a

The Road to El Palmar

week when it next starts up again.

Last night at the barbecue, a lady I was speaking to told me that there are three kinds of Levante wind and that Tarifa, though beautiful, has a high suicide rate because of it. Tarifa. Hmm. Maybe I should head down there tomorrow, just like I considered doing in the beginning before getting side-tracked by El Palmar. I could probably stay in Tarifa until it is time to return to Jerez. Maybe take a bus from there instead of heading back to Conil or Cadiz. It's an idea. Quite a few of the people I met at the party were from Tarifa, and they all seem to love it. That would leave me looking over the water to Africa, which could be fitting since it is likely the place I plan to go on the next trip, whenever that may be. Before I left to come out here I had an offer to go to Gambia and to a friend's drum compound there. I kind of pencilled it in for Xmas or New Year on a maybe.

So tomorrow I could cadge a lift off Pat when he goes to get supplies, and maybe find out if the buses go to Tarifa from Conil, and then find out from the *Touristica* just how to get to Jerez from Tarifa in one go later on. My money is stretching a bit thin now. Got less than 150 Euros left and have to pay for the board hire still. Expensive, since I hardly used it, but it was a good board. Only 7 foot and 8 inches long but it caught the small waves easily. I usually need a 10 footer for that, but this one was as good as any I have used before, and a lot lighter too. Nick said they only buy top boards for that reason. £450 a board, he said.

I am reflecting on what I found here at El Palmar. Maybe it is what anyone finds who travels and lets fate be the guide. It is the rhythm of life. Will I be back one day to make a home here? I doubt it. The feeling that I want to move on has firmly arrived today. Unexpected, but unmistakable. I am ready to move again, before I become too familiar with it and before the magic and mystery starts to fade. Maybe I will be back, I don't know. If I come into some money this year, or get the time and the urge to fly again next year. Maybe. Keep options open, and be ever ready to chop and change, that is the lesson I take from this journey. Make the plans, but if you can drop them again just as easily, then you are capable of flying and doing it right. Flexible enough to find all you need in each moment as it

The wind

unfolds. Undo the wires of sadness and longing that tie us down or into one place, to one world, to one perspective, and let the wind blow you where it may, or where you most deeply wish to go. It is sailing of a sort, and maybe at some level it is the wind that pushes you on when you travel like this. I felt like I heard it speak that night in Cadiz, when I first arrived and the Levante blew. I was on the rooftop, camped up there alone that night, and it whistled through my tent as I fell a sleep. Then it felt like I was half dreaming and in my half wake state I recall it seemed to keep telling me its name, S____m. I say the name now, because maybe it is time for it to take me on from here.

It's 2:30 pm and still the surf remains low, I continue to lie around and meditate in my tent. Finding the peace of internal silence as best I can and hold it for a while, enjoy the satisfaction of it. There is a wholeness comes from slowing down, a sense of timelessness, and it feels like a most natural state. I'm getting better at doing it with practice, and the siesta lends itself perfectly to that time because you don't have to be anywhere, see anyone, nor do anything. The day has barely begun by 2 pm in Spain, so it is a time when meditation is easy and acceptable. *This,* is exactly how I want to live. What I am doing, *right now*. Being, but not *doing* very much at all. In motion, not settled, just waiting for the wind to come and collect me and then blow me on to my next destination.

This is the person that I really am, not that creature back in London who is bound to the hamster wheel, running around in a shirt and tie all day, doing technical jobs for people who really could not give a damn about him at all. That's why this way seems so right, and also why it feels almost dangerous to consider. What I have left behind back there in London is not me at all. This is why I believe that I have found a part of myself out here, what a cliche that is, and yet... my mind entertains ways that could keep me on this path, because I want it and in many ways need it.

Yet as soon as I try to think about *the how*, any realistic idea just seems like it is distracting from the essence of what this path is really all about. The essence of freedom. The true way is not a planned one, but simply a way that is followed in the moment. There is no way to

The Road to El Palmar

plan for it, or build, or invest towards it, and that is the whole point. That is what makes it so challenging to trust in, to let go to, and to be on. It is a catch-22 in this respect. I need money to survive like this, and need to be able to make money to travel like this, but by making money, immediately I am back on the hamster wheel at some level.

How can I let go to this way of being, and just move around following the whim of each moment? Should I just become a bum? That idea terrifies me. I don't mind roughing it in a tent on the beach knowing that a meal, a shower, a comfortable bed and luxury surrounds are only a credit-card away, but I could not live like this. But then how on earth do I make enough money to survive without being in the rat-race? I do not have an answer yet.

Then I start to wonder, expand on ideas, and I get distracted. Would it be better with a truck than in a tent? Not really because that costs money too, trucks need up-keep, need road tax, need a place to park, need fuel, and so on and so forth. I reckon I could survive out here on 10 euros a day, excepting travel costs and luxuries, but even that is no good because I need to find a way to make a living while doing this. The only way that would really work, would have to be a passive-income source, so that it did not require my time nor energy.

I actually have no idea how to achieve this idealistic dream. It's been a question I have quietly been asking myself these last few years, ever since that trip to Newquay in 2002, and I still have not found any answers. Playing guitar, busking, it certainly has been fun to finally give it a go out here, but that won't really do it either. No one is interested enough to pay me for it, and it just doesn't come naturally for me to do music like that anyway. And I am no Paco de Lucia, that is for sure. Juan & Pat certainly made a point of letting me know that too. Though after one of Pat's monster cocktails, that he so loves to pass out around the bar and force upon anyone willing, almost anything seems possible.

I meditate a while longer, looking for my internal silence to offer up a key that might unlock the secret to this way of life. The Spirit needs to give me the answer, because it is the Spirit that would lead me on. The wind. The flow. Isn't that exactly what we mean by it? The Spirit of the journey guiding our every decision in the moment as we

The wind

flow with it. Following *the path with heart*, as Carlos Castaneda's Don Juan called it. The Spirit should be the power and the driving force behind all decisions and directional choices. Going with the flow. I don't know why, but the idea of it really doesn't feel all that natural to me currently. Is it stripped from our being by our time spent living in modernity? Maybe there is some art I have yet to learn or remember, some skill I have yet to discover that will make it all fall into place. It is as if the solution to this quandary is held back from me, maybe to ensure that I work to earn whatever it is that I need to learn.

There I go again, thinking it requires work. I am not sure it does, almost like the opposite is true. Stop *doing*, and start *being*. I guess I will know it when I am ready, because I do not find an answer now, not one that makes sense. I can't force the answer if it doesn't want to come. But I think that I know where it lies, and I know what I have to do to reach it. I have to keep trying to follow the Spirit in the moment. Get familiar with doing that, and trying to understand what that even means. Like in the book *The Alchemist,* that book is good in how it alludes well to this sense I am trying to grasp at here, though I have to say I find his other books a little bit sickly. This path I am on out here, I definitely tapped into something, to some brief sense of it for myself. I get what it is, I just do not yet know how to fully live it. I need to learn more. How to direct my life for the better, towards better things than just being locked into that damn nine-to-five for all eternity, a slave to a mortgage, the rat-race, my lifestyle choices, my addictions, my habits etc...etc... It's 3 pm, and I am still cooking here in the tent, time to go check the waves again.

I catch a few, but pretty soon find myself bored of it. My mind is elsewhere. I guess the question of what to do over the next two days is playing on my mind now, I have not made a firm decision yet. There is also a sense of resigned frustration, because soon I have to return to a world that has an annoying knack of making me unhappy. It didn't used to be that way, but it has become so of late. I think it is an age thing, maybe this is the start of my mid-life crisis. It is certainly harder to just be footloose and fancy free once you get older and less naive to the consequences. I can see no way to get on track with the spiritual

The Road to El Palmar

flow right now, and especially not back there in London. My earlier excitement at the idea has given way to an earth-bound reality. Soon I am going back to the machine, and I fear that I will forget what I have found out here.

I head back to the tent and roast in there until I discover that if I lift the side of the outer wrapping, then the breeze is able to cool me from the non-sunny side. Simple really, but I was nearly cooked-meat before I thought of doing it.

Now I seem to have entered a deflated impasse once again. Melancholia, with a hint of huffy. No wind whips in my sails, no ideas spring forth, no interest to move on, but no good reason to stay. I feel a familiar, age-old sense of sadness that reminds me of solitary days spent as a teenager at my Dad's flat in Bournemouth, sent there because divorce courts dictated that fathers should have time with their sons, I am not sure how much either of us particularly enjoyed that back then, but that was how it was. I would wander the beach alone and dream my Romeo dreams about future love, fame, and fortune. Days when such things had a curious way of being believable, the impossible seemed unquestioningly possible, the future simply looked bright, and yet teenage angst and tantrums were never very far away.

I hear a thud in the sand nearby. A couple of the local kids have turned up with bows and arrows and they loiter a distance from my tent. I found the makeshift arrows before, and figured someone had been using my tent for a spot of target practice. I bark a bit, maybe scare them off. Then just to be sure, I appear from the entrance and we eye one another. They wander off, unhappy that I have foiled their plan but before long comes another thud. This time it hits my tent! I guess they need to realise that I am a crazy and dangerous beach bum, and so like a moody old tramp I holler out.

"Rah! You little fuckers!"

I also don't think they realise that I recognise them from the bar. I will get their mum to give them a rollocking later on when I see her. See how the brats like it those bows and arrows. A kid's got to learn somehow and often best done the hard way to cement the lesson. Fear of the matriarch should do it. Can't blame them though, hassling bums is kind of fun as I remember it. In fact, I am surprised they held out

The wind

this long to launch an assault, I saw them wandering round with the weaponry a day ago.

I get out again, just to check that they really have gone this time. Last thing I need is a hole in my tent. They are walking away up the road, no doubt looking for easier victims. Though I notice a lot more arrows around my tent, and I realise they have probably been doing it for a lot longer than I thought. Jesus, it's like a goddamn Apache shooting range out here!

I have been writing and meditating for much of the day, but the melancholia hasn't lifted yet. I can't let go of the idea that I should somehow be living a more spiritual life, but I am at a loss as to what to do about that. Even if I had a realistic idea to aim towards, that would be something, but I don't. I only know that I am not happy back in London anymore. If I am honest with myself, I have painted myself into a corner and have no idea what to do about it. Twenty years ago, maybe even ten, I would have just burned it all to the ground, and then upped and left towards the first opportunity that presented itself. Back then it was easy to make those kinds of decisions. I moved to London on a whim in less than three days, I was nearly 23 years old at the time. I did not question it, I just went, and though it left a whole gamut of people behind me, including a distraught girlfriend, I knew it was the right thing to do at the time. Today, I actually don't know what to do. I have lost touch with the part of myself that could make decisions in that way. It's as if I have become institutionalised. Been in full-time employment since I was 27, one way or another. I have become a careerist. Most people are content with that. For some reason, I am not.

I will maybe try and avoid getting drunk again tonight, and instead take some time out here on the beach. Stare at the black night and the ocean and meditate some more. I am now feeling pretty certain this will be my last day in El Palmar. I have a feeling that staying in this spot will not remain so secluded either, more and more people keep passing by my tent to find some place to relieve themselves on the beach.

The kids return, and I give them a verbal dressing down. They say

The Road to El Palmar

they didn't do anything. I roll my eyes with a 'whatever' and then finish my speech. That sorted, they just give each other looks. I didn't manage to command quite the level of respect that I had hoped for. I wonder if I could get away with drowning one of them as a message to the others. Probably not. Bored little vermin that they are. I get it. I wanted to destroy things at their age, in fact I still want to destroy things. I guess I should be grateful that none of them seem to be taking up an interest in pyromania as well. Flaming arrows would be a very bad escalation of events. They finally huff off again, and I watch them go.

I am a stranded, castaway, caught in the doldrums, yes I am. Temperature still high down here in the tent, camped in the bushes on the beaches of El Palmar currently under the threat of attack by tooled-up midget Spanish infidels. The open side brings some relief from the heat and allows me to watch for the further launching of volleys from the enemy. I get back to my musing.

How am I going to afford to travel like this without earning money? The problem always comes down to money. My life, perforce, has to be devoted to making the damn stuff. There is no way, that I can see, to devote myself to the spirit of travel unless I can afford to travel. I think it was Lao Tzu who said that enlightenment is not possible without a large amount of money, because you need other people to look after all the admin duties, while you meditate yourself into a being of light. That kind of devotion to it is a long way off for me, and I am not sure it is my bag anyway. I don't know how to become a monk nor a fully-fledged bum. I'll think on it some more. Surely there must be an answer, even if I cannot yet grasp what it is.

I go back to my meditating and the next time I come up for air, I realise that in a funny way one answer has been staring me in the face all day. It is all about functioning immediately. I have been sat considering moving on and sat questioning it all. Then it hits me - the fact that I am considering moving on, is the call itself. I have been procrastinating. So, I am now toying with the idea of moving on tonight. I feel I am actually ready to go right now, which is maybe what has been bothering me. A nagging feeling, ever since I mentioned using the wind to call me on, and it takes me a few hours to realise that

The wind

maybe it called me immediately. That, is the nagging feeling. It is actually time to go, and right now. Why wait at all?

An idea forms. I could hang about here until the sun is nearly down, then head back along the beach towards Conil, tent up in the dark along that part of the beach just before the town. It's backed only by tufty lumps of inhospitable grassland and that big, empty tower thing, so I should not have a problem with anyone coming along. Then, in the morning, get up and catch an early bus to Tarifa. I am making assumptions that there is such a thing. But I am a little loathed to move. I guess that is my natural rooting system starting to settle in here, but something also tells me that I should go, that it is time.

People keep spotting me tented up here now, that is new, until today I pretty much saw no one down here on the beach. I don't want the Civil Guardia's bows and arrows coming at me next. Yes, I am finally decided - it is time to move on. I'll have to go and bid my farewells to the good people that I have met here, and leave some money for Nick in payment for the surf equipment too. I am certain now. It's time to go. 7:20 pm. I better get started.

On the road again

I left El Palmar that evening just as the sun was getting low. Stopping by So-Co bar just as Nick and Gary showed up. They offered me again the chance to go with them to the west coast of Portugal. To the southern part, just below Lisbon. I politely declined. I was sure now that I was headed for Tarifa to finish off my trek down the south-west coast of Spain. Portugal, I would have to save for another time. A future adventure, and maybe better prepared after all that I have learnt here. Bring a truck, or maybe a camper-van, or maybe not.

I had noticed that you can park up along the coast indefinitely in El Palmar, or so it seemed. Some vans were doing just that further down, and had been there long before I got situated and pitched up on the beach.

So I sat at the bar in So-Co for a while, taking it all in. Lisa, Pat's sister, was back in. It turned out she had been ill, which is why she hadn't shown up since the first day, and she said hello, and then we enter into animated conversation. It was curious, as in my last moments there, I was finally getting a glimpse into the darker side of everyone's story. She told me about a paedophile barman, and one of the lads having fist fights with various people in the bar. I found her even easier to talk to than the others, and it struck me that the conversation just flowed naturally when I was with certain types of people. Usually those willing to tell the truth as they see it, and not just some narrative. I also found what she told me really interesting, not least because it made a few things fall into place that I had not been able to figure out, but had picked up on. The underlying tensions and the politics, those things that you never see until you live in a place, but you somehow sense it in the people, maybe as reticence or a stand offish nature, but you can't quite put your finger on what it is. I had a lot of *aha* moments listening to her. It wasn't like the dream was shattered, or some romantic notion that I had put upon the place was lifted. It was more like the reality that I had intuited anyway, was given

On the road again

confirmation. I preferred to keep my time in El Palmar as magical, and in order to do that, I now had to leave. It seemed to have all timed itself perfectly, and with the final bits of information from Lisa just putting a bow around the top, I could see the blue-print of it all laid out across the entire story as it finally unfolded for me.

So, I bid farewell and gave a big thanks to Pat. He was sat with two interesting looking English guys, one was missing a finger and had something wrong with his shoulder. They were friendly, but seemed pretty tough, I liked them immediately. Pat offered to give me a lift to Jerez if I got stuck, and so I took his email address and phone number just in case. Then in those last moments I felt an incredible ache begin in me. It was so intense, that I thought I was about to burst into tears, something that never happens to me. Christ, I had only known these people for a few days! I knew that I had to get going before it got any worse. They say the best goodbye is a quick one, and so I made my exit.

As I began my walk up the beach from the edge of El Palmar and northward back towards Conil, that intense emotion dispelled quite quickly. I was back on the trail again, moving and solitary, I had a destination and that gave me purpose, and it felt good. At one point I turned to look back. Out on the rocks that stick out from El Palmar, right there by the tall tower, I could make out a few figures, and one was waving. Involuntarily, I started waving back. I genuinely thought they had all come out to wave me off. As I squinted, I realised it was just the waves and the shape of the rocks there. I felt stupid at my emotional reaction and stopped waving as the wash of shame flowed over me. But it made me wonder if maybe there is a parallel universe where people just know without asking, show their feelings for one another without fearing it, know one another intimately and immediately, some kind of parallel state where such things as making a fool of yourself are all simply okay. And I wondered if they were feeling it too, what mark I had left behind me if any. I felt an inconsolable sorrow. It was bigger than just leaving El Palmar, it was for all the moments that I had left behind me. Like when you meet people briefly, and you both feel an intensely strong connection. That

The Road to El Palmar

perfect first moment before anything much is known about each other. You sense in the midst of the vast ocean we call time and eternity that something real is happening between you both. Then just as quickly as it arrives, it is gone. Everything becomes normalised and the magic fades until it is used up. You never get to know what that was.

There is an incredible sadness in moving on, and yet everyone has to eventually. Love must become grief at some point, it's just the journey we are on. But there is also a sense of incredible possibilities, that's what you feel with some people on that first brief moment of meeting them, you know there is something incredible in it just beyond our reach. I felt it then, and I also felt the impossible nature of its transience too. As I stood there on the beach thinking about it all, I knew that it might overwhelm me with the power of it's longing if I stayed in it too long. So I turned, and continued on along that desert-like expanse that connects El Palmar to Conil. It was another familiar feeling, I realised, to always be moving on. All my life I have been doing it one way or another, having to say goodbye.

As the sun hit the horizon I made camp by the middle tower, about half way between the two towns. There was not another living thing out there in that desolate expanse, except for me, and the midges, and the night. I slept with the tent open, but with the mesh net up. It all looked quite Moroccan somehow, the way the sand stretched away down to the sea, and the crescent moon hung with the stars in the sky like some nomadic tapestry scene. It was printed in light, up there in the tent entrance, a triangular aperture framing it. It was all far too perfect to be real. As if a god was laughing at my stupidity for not realising that such grandiose views could never have simply happened by accident. I am not sure why it portrayed such a beautiful image, nor why I felt so exquisitely solitary as I did that night. It wasn't loneliness at all, it was far beyond that, rather it was more like finally finding a deep peace within myself, a peace that I had lost since growing up and becoming an adult. The rest of the world didn't exist for me that night, it was completely washed away, and above it all I felt intensely aware of what it meant to be alive. I felt honoured to have finally been able to grasp that, and it felt curiously easy and simple to do as I did. An inexplicable joy stayed with me until I fell asleep. I felt connected to

On the road again

the universe by it, no longer concerned that I was alone, no longer hungering for something that I could not put my finger on, no longer in need, nor longing for anything much at all, there was just a sense of an untroubled peace that I had been longing to find all along. I was on the road again.

Nights in white satin, never reaching the end

I finally did a bit of Tai-chi before bedding down on the beach between El Palmar and Conil. The first time I had been alone enough to do it and not feel embarrassed about being seen. I slept for a good ten hours, though it wasn't as comfortable as El Palmar's sand it was noticeably harder.

I awoke at 8:30 am and got out of the tent to stretch. There was no wind, and I was feeling good until I spotted dark clouds to the south. I was a mile away from shelter. Not knowing how long the rains might stay for if they arrived, and seeing that they were headed my way, I dropped camp quickly and began a fast gait across the hard packed sand with my stuffed ruck-sack, guitar in hand, and just flip-flops on my feet. I was not sure I could make it to Conil before the rains, but I needed to try. At times I was almost running as the land behind me began to disappear, consumed by the darkness of threatening skies and the rainfall that was no doubt landing on El Palmar. It had been a smart choice to leave.

I reached Conil and relaxed my pace, but then realised that I still had the torment of the climb up its hilly streets to get to the centre and to the tourist office. I huffed and puffed my way up the final stretch only to discover that the office was closed until 9:30 am. I wasn't going to catch any 9 am bus after all. So I went to a nearby coffee shop, and while I was in there the rain began to fall on Conil. My body was aching, adjusting to the shock I had just given it.

I was back in a relatively civilised town, and looking even more like a tramp. Funny how it doesn't even register when you are in a place that you feel at home such as El Palmar. I had even more matted hair and the white t-shirt was stained yellow by the sun-tan lotion. I tried to tidy myself up a bit in the toilets but the sweat of the morning run had not helped, there was not much I could do about my state. I felt like an outcast to be this way, and not for the first time. I checked my cash and discovered I had 80 euros left.

Nights in white satin, never reaching the end

Lisa told me that she had left England with massive debts, two kids, and just 600 euros, money that she was still living on, so she said. She had left back in September. I found it hard to believe that was all the money she had, but she assured me that the bar hadn't earned them anything yet, and that she still had some of that money left. She said that debts didn't follow you out to Spain, and that she would never want to go back anyway. I believed her sincerity, but I knew from experience that eventually she'd regret the decision to burn her bridges. People always want to go back home at some point. Sometimes, when we cut ourselves off from our past, that sense of it being a home for us becomes more apparent and almost hallucinatory, maybe in part due to the fact it is then denied to us. I think that women especially end up drawn back to the parental nest, possibly more so than men. All the same, the determination of the ex-pats that I met in El Palmar fascinated and amazed me in equal measure. All of them had dropped their lives with apparent ease, to take up a piece of the sea-and-surf lifestyle, and all of them had kids that they either brought with them or had there. It was inspirational for me to see people living like that, making those kind of changes and sacrifices.

I had seen it in Nicaragua too, but out there they were mostly North American ex-pats and their experiences did not resonate with me in the same way that El Palmar's inhabitants had. I had to admit it was clearly possible to make the kind of changes that they had done, regardless of their situation or how difficult they thought it might be. They were the living proof. However hard it looked, it was always possible to sacrifice everything and just go. All their stories were the same, almost everyone I spoke to, of deciding that the UK was no good for them anymore, then simply getting on a plane with no real idea how they would survive, and just leaving. Working it out as they went along. They were undeniably happy in their new lives at some level because they were engaged in working towards whatever it was that brought them to be there in the first place. They were literally *living the dream*, however hard that dream was to create in reality, they were in the place they wanted to be and working towards it.

Obviously there were issues, and they all had history and personal problems that had followed them out there, but who doesn't have

The Road to El Palmar

problems of some sort? There was no sign of regret, but no pretence that they were in paradise either. And even if I had been stoically cynical of their claimed successes - which I wasn't - it was impossible not to let the feeling sweep me up and be impressed by it. They were living their dreams, and those dreams were keeping them busy, and the journey towards that end was clearly a satisfying one. Not like my life spent in an over-priced shoe-box, with a life-long mortgage and drowning in debts, while feeling trapped, and damned, and with nothing left to do but complain endlessly about it into Word documents. They had all sacrificed the allegedly *safe option* that we all go in for back home, swapped it for the risks of adventure and freedom. It was certainly a huge challenge, and no doubt kept many of them awake at night, but it gave them their zest for life too. There was a genuine happiness that I had witnessed there. They had joined up with others just like them, to fight to achieve something together. I had happened upon the starting of a fine little ex-pat community in El Palmar. People who liked to surf, and took occasional road-trips together, families who lived on plots of land, not in houses, but in caravans or run down old motor homes. The land serving as an investment for the future, while avoiding the huge outlay of a plot with a house on the grid. No one minded the gypsy way of life in El Palmar, maybe because to some extent there was not much choice. There was no infrastructure to cater to the demands of urban living. Not yet, at least. But with El Palmar being the preferred holiday spot of many a native Spaniard every year, it was not a stupid investment at all, but really quite a smart one.

    Everything in El Palmar was in the early stages of a period of growth. It was exactly what I went to Nicaragua expecting to find, but found something else instead. Con artists mostly, and a town trying to achieve what neighbouring Costa Rica had already achieved and the price had sky-rocketed there accordingly. Nicaragua was unable to progress in the way that I hoped because it was not yet ready for it and that showed. You could sense the desperation beneath the crocodile smiles of the real estate agents that licked their lips every time someone new and green showed up in town. Nicaragua had yet to recover from the Sandinista revolts of the eighties, for better of for worse the re-

Nights in white satin, never reaching the end

allocation of land ownership had just muddied the clarity around property rights. Those issues were just the beginning. There were also the 19 active volcanoes to consider, and the tendency for coastal towns to disappear under a tsunami every now and then. Where I was looking at buying land this was definitely a problem no one mentioned. There were many other problems too, and it did not take the five days that I was there for a lot of them to become apparent. But in El Palmar there is no sense of danger, not at that same level of uncertainty. Death is not quite so prevalent there, nor is it lurking behind the offers that you are given. Maybe it is there, certainly it is there, but escape from it is just a short drive away. The dream to find land where I might escape modernity, a place to live in as it grew up gradually, had become shelved after the failure of my Nicaraguan trip. Now it had unexpectedly re-awakened.

As I sit here now, and wait to begin the final part of my journey, I see that all this boils down to is one simple question - *do I want a piece of this?* Because if I do, then there is very little reason for me not to close down all that I have in England and head out here. These guys stand as testament to the fact that it can be done, whatever your life situation. If you have had enough of it all, then all it really takes is a decision. Simply drop everything and leave.

It is too soon for me to take it in properly, but I am definitely tempted by its lure. It creates excitement in me to think on it, and I do so miss feeling excited by life. If I came out here, I could become a part of what is developing in this small community. It is not all that far for my friends to come visit either. What would I bring to it? What would I want to develop here for myself? What part would I play here? Even if it just began as some kind of investment and I stayed in the UK at first, that would be a good start. Travel out here when I had the time, maybe even live half the year here in Spain and the other half earning money back in the UK somehow. It's so much cheaper here, and could easily be that way for maybe another five or ten years to come. This part of south-west Spain seems far less tourist infested, though I am here early in the season.

It will change, of course. I have seen the effects of that change,

The Road to El Palmar

like with the development going on back in Conil near the camp site, but that all has a long way to go to become anything like Malaga, or Benidorm, or any of the other well-trod tourist locations. And El Palmar, even more remote and cut-off than Conil. How long can it last that way if it is a Spanish holiday hot-spot? They don't currently have full water service, nor proper electricity, nor the benefits of modern urbanisation enough for it to interest the big spenders and the hotel conglomerates, but it is surely coming. I passed building works on the drive out with Pat on that first day. He showed me where they are putting water pipes in for El Palmar's first hotel.

My spirit feels roused by the urge to come and enjoy El Palmar while it still retains a sense of unmodernised wildness. To buy a piece of it as an investment might be smart, however much I hate being a part of that inevitable monster-truck of modernisation, where builders, architects, money-men, and developers all come to raze the land, kill the culture, and replace nature with concrete and ATM machines, but there is little point in being a hippy about it all. No one ever stopped modernisation, and the march of progress moves ever on. The truth is, such things have their benefits too. Which reminds me, I need to find an ATM and get some more money out before I leave here.

I find one, but of course, it isn't giving out any money. But the *Touristica* is now open, and there I discover that there are no buses from Conil to Tarifa until 7 am tomorrow, so I decide to make for Cadiz again instead. I will catch the 10:45 am bus that goes there, and hopefully I can head to Tarifa later today from Cadiz on a bus that I am told should be running. The sky is trying to clear though it remains somewhat cloudy, but the rain has eased off for now.

As if to seal the deal with El Palmar, I spot Julian across the road while I am waiting for the bus. The crazy, long-haired guitarist from the other night who liked to wear shades at night time. He comes over, and we chat until my bus shows up. He tells me that he rents a place out near Colorado, but has just had a windfall from his Nan and is now dealing with the paperwork involved in buying a place. He is a really likable guy, and is so laid-back it makes me want to laugh whenever I speak with him.

Nights in white satin, never reaching the end

"We'll see you again, right?" He asks me.

"I hope so." I reply, and step aboard my bus.

I can't deny what this place has done for me. Can a place want you? Or is it just coincidence or our own sense of bias, that appears around us like omens and signs that seem to say - *maybe a good future lies in wait for you here*. I've tried to do many things with my life, and one thing I have found is that no matter how hard you try to do something, it only ever really works out if it is already supposed to. You simply can't force some things to work out unless they are willing. It is how I approached many opportunities that have presented themselves and to date this has always held true. It is also, conversely, the most likely reason why I have never got anywhere with music. It is just not meant to be, and it is certainly not from want of trying. Music has been an endless up-hill struggle and doors rarely opened in the way I wanted them to, though they opened in unexpected ways I must admit. It is why I feel that this place now invites me to return, it is making it very easy for me to do so. No one teaches us about this approach to opportunity when we are in school, instead they teach us the concept that everything must be hard work. I don't think that is right at all, some things just flow, and often the best things come to us in that way. *The Alchemist* book touches on this approach, as does *The Celestine Prophecy* by James Redfield. Though in a counterpoint to it, I recall a bit of graffiti that I saw in an Amsterdam cafe once that said - *only dead fish go with the flow*.

If this *going with the flow* method is a better way of dealing with opportunity and progress through life - which I suspect it is - then that would suggest that there is a path for us that is already laid out. It may actually be many paths, but when we are on one that wants us then it will run smoothly and unfold easily, with obvious signs along the way. We fit onto it like a train fits onto rails. We turn where we are supposed to turn, and go past what we are supposed to go past when we are supposed to go past it. It all runs quite simply and easily, when the road fits us well.

But if we are on the wrong path then it fights us. We chase mental desires that are beyond our reach, get caught up in mental aberrations, over-reach mental ambitions, and then it's a hard uphill struggle that

The Road to El Palmar

seems to make us sweat for nothing. It has taken me years to understand this truth, even theoretically, and for the last few years I have been floundering in exactly that kind of failure. I know I am on the wrong path, the problem is that I do not know how to get off it. Where once I knew exactly how to follow a *path with heart*, but now fear, sense of duty, and habitual routine all conspire to keep me trapped on what feels like the wrong rails. We can most certainly dig grooves on the wrong roads for ourselves, I have done it, and it makes it all the harder to get off them again when we know that we should. I can attest to that method of failure. I suspect that many of us can, because it seems to get harder with age and not easier at all. Change comes at least once or twice into our lives in a big way, and paths end. Good paths then become wrong paths. I am thinking of the miners of North England in the eighties as I write this line, they did not know how to change direction when the good path beneath their feet changed to bad. This is one example in life where the youth have an advantage, because they have a total lack of experience on their side, they are too young to realise how dangerous their choices might be, and they have not had time to become deeply attached to the path that they have been on. Age makes it more difficult to make that change, and we are far more willing to live with pain that we are familiar with experiencing.

The beauty of doing what I have done this holiday, by taking the leap out and then just freewheeling into the hands of fate, is that I have been able to flex the muscle in me that I once used to follow a *path with heart*. I have had nothing to stop me testing making choices here, other than the voices in my head, so it has been easy to find my flow again. I have been free to go with the flow and to observe how to make my decisions in a moment-by-moment way, instead of planning it all out ahead of time. A planned future leaves no room for the Spirit to enter in and direct our flow.

But I see something else too. Throughout school, and throughout our subsequent years as careerists, we have learnt to be afraid of the unknown, to fear change. Following the Spirit is the opposite of what we have been taught to do, and is the opposite of what we are encouraged to do. We are encouraged to insure against trouble, play

Nights in white satin, never reaching the end

safe, plan well and invest for a well-defined future. We are told this is the safest way, but is it? I feel far from safe and secure back in London, I feel more fear than ever since I got a mortgage, because there is always some new, more powerful fear that manages to threaten my sense of security. And now it feels more like a trap. Yet this way I am functioning out here - despite stinking like a pole-cat and looking like a vagrant - actually feels far more natural to me than shaving daily, and suiting-up to be a well-oiled cog in the IT machine. This way, I actually feel alive. Fear and habitual inertia now account for a lot of my choices back home. In fact our entire culture runs on it, just look at the News reports that feed us. Greed, Fear and Apathy run modernity, and it's a future that is mortgaged out.

Though our conditioned method is hard to let go of, I think I have now managed to capture something of the process of letting go. I know how to do it, because I actually just did it. Just for a moment I broke free. I guess it is about learning to trust that quiet inner voice, the one that never speaks very loudly but never shuts up either, and thank god. It pops up whenever we have a decision to make, and simply says - *don't go that way, do that other crazy thing instead.* Our minds then get lost in the dilemma of assessing everything, but I think another part of us knows immediately what is what. Though one could argue, that is exactly what gets people into trouble, and they might be right, but there lies the rub. Even so, it's been a beautiful lesson and experience, and one that I hope I will be able to sustain and not forget.

In trying to define some aspects of it now, I think one trick is in being able to reverse your most firm decisions in an instant. It is not easy to do that. City life is going to try to wipe it from me again, I know that much. It will only take a day or two being back, before I will look at this time with a curious question of whether I actually just went mad. I write this now to remind myself what I saw out here. Going mad is sometimes good for us.

There are those people with the ability to drop everything, sacrifice everything, cling to nothing, and then walk out of their lives and walk away from the past forever. It is possible, however wrong we may perceive that act to be, and sometimes it is necessary. There is actually nothing stopping us following our dreams other than our thoughts.

The Road to El Palmar

Maybe we should, or maybe we shouldn't, that is not actually the point. To *act* is what matters, and to act requires just one decision.

Then there is the Spirit, the fates, luck, opportunity, the gods, or the goddamn baby Jesus, whatever you wish to call it - when the path reverses on itself, as it did with me yesterday, then we must be capable of following it as it shifts. It called for me to leave yesterday, and I dithered in making that decision, which then caused more dithering until I spotted my error. That, is the flow. It is never in a straight and convenient line. The path often reverses on itself very rapidly, and then suddenly it is gone from beneath our feet. That is the moment we have to become tuned in to. That is the art of evolution and survival. We have to learn how to see it, to recognise it, and then to slow ourselves down enough to hear that small voice inside us, because it is telling us which way to go in order to re-connect with the Spirit. It is telling us how to follow *a path with heart,* and nobody knows that better than our own little voice.

I just re-read that paragraph, and I think it is right. Hopefully I will understand it again when I am chained to my desk at the office, being chewed-out for not doing enough work and wondering what the hell just happened, and where my mojo went. Completely forgetting, as I will, that it is a self-made prison, and that I could actually walk out of there at any time, if only I had the balls.

Our emotional reaction, our personal insecurities, our sense of doubt, and our confusions, all work against that inner *knowing*. We have let go of our natural ability to flow with life. We have become fearful of it. Everyone has fear in modernity, and without the support of our fellow human beings, it is always going to be much harder to achieve. Which makes me think about another aspect of this - a monkey not behaving according to the Simian order generally creates fear in the other monkeys. Those other monkeys will then do anything in their power to stop that one monkey from misbehaving. Fear and emotional terrorism are powerful devices in monkey world, and hairless monkeys are the worst perpetrators of the aggressive application of order.

Of course, even the *path with heart* inevitably leads us on to our final moment on earth, and maybe that is why we must face our fears along the way. In the end we have no choice at all, not really. Is this

Nights in white satin, never reaching the end

why we are here? To experience this powerlessness and learn how to navigate in spite of it? The fact of the matter is we *are* here, and we have no choice but to ride the journey of our lives that inevitably includes going through jaws at the end. Nothing is changing that factuality. Our only choice is how we spend our time here, assuming we really have any free choice at all.

There is no feeling to compare with knowing that you are on the right road. For me, that is what freedom means. I felt it last night, as I tented down on the beach between El Palmar and Conil. The star in the sky shining through the aperture of my tent held it for me. Everything felt complete, and everything felt okay. There was not even a question, in fact there was no fear at all. It was probably the first time this trip that I felt a total relief from the nagging anxiety that dogs me. It is currently the piece of the jigsaw that is missing from my understanding on all this. Something needs to help me lift that anxiety that I live with constantly, and I felt free of it in that moment last night. I was caught in a lull, maybe in part because I felt half-way between new adventures. Moving on seems to bring with it an elusive confidence.

My heart and mind seem to be fairly content right now, much more than they have been back home of late. Out here I feel like I own nothing at all, and as a result *nothing* owns me. Those mortgages, debts, relationships, and ties, are all just gestures from another time, an hallucination that is not as real as it pretends to be. The only thing that is real, is the power that brought me to be in this life and pushes me on through it still, and if I let go to it, then it might well guide me on. I just have to remember how to listen to its gentle, soft call, then pick up it's alluring invite to follow.

We reach Cadiz and pass Cortadura. It seems so long ago that I struggled with dark moods there. The Moody Blues play on the coach radio, and it's a number that I cover in my set at the moment - *Nights in white satin*. I can feel the music in me again, and that feels pretty good.

I have a slightly embarrassing confession to make, though I am not sure why it feels embarrassing at all. Last night after my Tai-Chi session, while alone on that long, flat expanse of beach and as the darkness began to descend, there under the moon and the stars, I sang to the Spirit. I begged for it to finally descend on me, and to make some kind of sense and not let me forget it this time. Then I tried to let go of everything inside me, to become blank and internally quiet. I played and sang, and after a while managed to lose myself in the expression, I let go to the music. Then, in the midst of this attempt at having a moment, my strap popped off the guitar. I swear it felt like something had just touched me, and I was swinging around in the dark looking for some culprit, ready for the fight. There was no one there.

I return to Cadiz with a renewed sense of confidence, less uncertainty and more strength and determination than I possessed when I was here last. It serves as a good reference point. Coming back here now, it makes me aware just how much I have been through these last few days, tempered by the sea and the spirit of El Palmar.

I check the Tarifa bus-timetable and it is good news, I have only 2 hours to kill before it leaves. For some reason I am still not hungry, though I haven't eaten since yesterday afternoon. I make for the Church square to have a quick go at busking. I was so afraid of doing it before I went to El Palmar, but there is a lot less fear in me now that I have broken the ice. I choose a spot away from the cafes and on a busy walkway entrance just below a tree in case the sun comes out again. After the bells of the church finish off their chimes, this place - the point that I entered south-west Spain and where my adventure started - is where I officially begin my busking debut.

Inspired by the coach trip radio, I start with *Nights in white satin,* and it earns me my first euro. After 30 minutes more of various numbers from my repertoire I have earned only one more coin, but I don't care. I am just happy to finally be doing what I came here to do. I now know that I can play like this anywhere and anytime. I have busking under my belt at long last. I have done it. This is a special moment for me.

A little while later, I find an Internet cafe and write an email to let her know all is well. I am brief but also let her know where I am bound for the last leg of my journey. Then I return to the bus station to wait the short time before my bus leaves for Tarifa. The sun is only now

Nights in white satin, never reaching the end

starting to break through. I still don't feel hungry, though I know I should probably eat anyway. I grab a coffee, write into my notebook to catch up with events, and then head off to get my bus ticket. The sweat of carrying my luggage is now giving me considerable discomfort, but my body and mind are resigned to the journey on, and I am happy.

Is this really who I am now?

I am on the bus to Tarifa and just passing Conil again. Then we cut through the pass into the mountains behind Vejer de la Frontera, the town that looks down on El Palmar. I have been wondering throughout the bus journey about how to get out here, why I would come, the drive behind my reasoning, the underlying reasons to do it, and what they would be?

I pass signs of progress and civilisation. El Palmar has only got so long before the arrival of hotels, and with it the problems of modernity and tourism shall begin. I see no escape for it in the long-term, and my mind begins to wonder if maybe I should look just outside of El Palmar for land there. In this train of thought I again feel a little uncomfortable. I don't really want to keep finding ways to get locked into more possessions and ownership. I need to keep reminding myself that, tempting as it is, this is the whole reason I am in a pickle in the first place. Ownership doesn't seem to work well for me. It leaves me in a state of distress. This journey I am on is about the Spirit, it is about living in the moment, engaging in something other than purchases, loans, bricks, mortar, fields, donkeys, trucks, mobile homes, and possessions for cash.

I stop thinking along those lines, and try to meditate again. *Do not struggle for the answers, learn to let them come.* A short while later, I am looking out of the window at mountains and realise that there is a way to delay, and sometimes avoid, progress and civilisation by going to the mountains. Generally mountains hold back the invasion of modernity. They are too rugged, too inhospitable, too difficult to traverse and dig about in, it is hard to build and concrete over a mountain. Not impossible, but generally they make it a lot more challenging. Of course you get towns in mountains, and motorways too, and rail-roads and pipelines cut through them, but it is a lot harder to modernise, and civilise a mountain village. I think this is true, so I take a note of it and then return to meditating.

Is this really who I am now?

We move out beyond the low mountains of Vejer, and the backdrop of nature gives way to what looks like man-made orchards and square farmland, much like what I saw from the plane. The rains start to fall again quite hard, and I find myself thinking that maybe next time I should buy a horse and travel with nothing but a poncho. The tent is too big to make travel with it comfortable, a big hat would have done as much for me in this warmth, even with the rains.

It's hard to see the land here now that the rain has created a misty veil obscuring much beyond the edge of the road. I catch glimpses of quarries, and then orchards that are not so pretty in their uniformity. I could be in England with the green grass and this rain. I find myself thinking about buying land again. It would be cheaper out here, and El Palmar is a fairly short distance from this area. I wonder where I am headed now, and what lies in store at Tarifa. The rains are falling harder, and I am heading further into them. The land is relatively hilly around these parts. We must be some way south of El Palmar by now and maybe inland a bit. The fields covered in grass look a lot less dry. I wonder if it rains more around here, though I don't understand why it would. The mountains might cause it I suppose, and air coming in off the sea. There is more land than there are buildings. It actually reminds me a bit of Wiltshire in England. Some fields full of horses, others with sunflowers, most just full of grass. And now a large flat expanse, dead and empty, and made more so by the electrical pylons that run across it. The concrete progression that man, by default, drives ceaselessly on towards achieving. I want to fight it, turn it around. But to hate it, or war against progress makes no real sense either. You need to find a balance, need to create a place where nature can flourish and spread out, like a cure for the metal and concrete before it becomes a world consumed by it all.

Some burnt out trees from old bush fires which may explain why this land is so empty. Wild-fires are not something I have to think about in England, so there is something else to watch out for if coming out here. Mountains in the distance, maybe to the east. The rain clearing a little now.

I hope Tarifa will not be a damper on expectations after the

The Road to El Palmar

wonderful time had in El Palmar. I felt I needed to come this way all the same, complete the journey, it was no mistake. Even if only to know what lies south of El Palmar.

Fields of corn. Ready for harvest soon by the look of it, yet it is only May. Gigantic wind turbines out there to the west. Huge stalks nesting in the tops of pylons. Boy, I am hungry now. I am wondering on ways to make money. Legal or otherwise. I consider ideas, not all are salubrious. A guy I met at the bar in El Palmar called Bik, he made me laugh.

"The universe isn't predatory, it is parastatitical," he said.

He meant *parasitical* but was adding in an extra *stat*. I didn't correct his pronunciation. I liked his extended word, it gave it a nice rhythm, but besides that, I thought it was quite a profound comment. The more I considered it, the more I realised that he was right. As we start the drive into Tarifa itself, it isn't as I expected. In fact it appears pretty ugly.

We enter in past concrete squares, large block high-rises, maybe ten storeys high. The best word for it is *eye-sore*. It's one long road in, past kite-surf shops, and kite-surf shops, and… more kite-surf shops. I see cool dudes, and lots of English-looking white folk. Where the hot blazes is the Moroccan and African contingent in this place? This is not like in *The Alchemist* at all.

I am off the bus, and check to confirm my journey back. Good news, I can go straight from here to Jerez at 10:30 am tomorrow. I have been told it is nice in the old-town at Jerez and the thought of it being horse-centric appeals to me. It isn't on the coast, so I was going to skip staying there originally, but plans change as they need to, and I have to fly out of there back to London anyway.

I stroll into a fake Mexican food-bar close by and order up a burrito veggie-style. Two annoying English ex-pats sit two seats away, they seem to be a couple. He, the type you expect in Benidorm, and her, a plump, gold-jangling, sparkly-eyed-in-the-wrong-kind-of-way businesswoman. I dislike their type instinctively and try to avoid eye contact but can't avoid their loudness. This does not bode well for the kind of people that I might find in Tarifa. They are busy going to work

Is this really who I am now?

on a white, well fed, and rich looking lady. I guess they are real-estate agents going in for the kill. It dawns on me that this isn't the first time I have disliked people like them on sight. I listen to him work it. Lather the bullshit. All that *talk, talk, talk*. Like crocodiles, interested only in the money of this dumb, large lady's investment account. I reprimand myself for being so judgemental, but it does little good, I know that these are not my people and I know the game. It is what makes the world go round, so I am told. I don't want to be in here listening to their cheap sales-pitch, so I hurry up and finish. It was seven euros for my food, and it was encouragingly good despite my concern about a faux-Mexican restaurant in the South of Spain. The owner, moody looking upon entry, now smiles at me as I leave. Maybe he did not think I would pay. I forget that I look like a bum. This change of heart from the owner, makes me feel a bit less critical of the place. I now have some energy to carry on and find the centre, see what Tarifa is all about.

I find a map on a street stand and check it out. No camping listed, but there is a tourist office. I head for that, only to find it closed. Then I head to the beach to discover that it is quite ugly and grubby looking, maybe there is another one somewhere. It is not helped by the post-rain overcast skies I don't suppose, but it wouldn't be a patch on where I have just been even if it was sunny. The beach backs onto what looks like swamp land. The place is weird, why do people come here. If anyone wished to invade Spain, come to Tarifa at 3 pm because no one will notice, it's empty.

I stroll like a hunch-back with my pack, on up the beach, checking out places for a potential camp spot. It does not look safe around here. I decide to look for a hostel instead, and soon end up almost back where the bus dropped me. I don't feel at ease here like I did in El Palmar and Cadiz. I also don't feel too safe leaving my belongings anywhere, and without booking a hostel, I will have to stay close to wherever I camp. So hostel it is, at least for tonight, just so I can dump all this crap and take a look around.

I pick one called *No Work Team*. Weird name, but I like it. Expecting Aussies, I find only a Spanish lady. It is 15 euros for the night and the outer door is open at 8 am, I accept the rules without

The Road to El Palmar

really listening. Though I don't like that she keeps my passport with no receipt, something I later learn never to do, but she caught me on the hop and insisted. I figure she won't be going anywhere and I certainly won't be leaving without it. While she fills out some forms on my behalf, I watch the Prince of Spain's wedding on TV. I had no idea that Spain has a royal family. How very lovely.

I find Room 16. Which reminds me of a song called *Puppet Life* by Punishment of Luxury. The opening words go -

"Here they come, they'll never take me away, I wont go to room 16." [other voice] *"You will, you're already theeeeeeeeerrrree!"*

I have no idea why I told you that.

My room is compact and bijou for the price and the window looks out onto the main street from the first floor. There is a toilet and bathroom somewhere but not in here clearly, I have a quick look outside but can't see them, for now I wash in the sink and then re-pack my rucksack. I get rid of some of the sand that is in there. I find another pen, my last two have run out, maybe it is the heat.

The rains have left Tarifa, but the clouds haven't. So far it is an ugly town to me. Too much cheap concrete, a crapola beach, badly painted architecture, low socio-economic housing at the beach, and just too many kite-surf shops. But I keep an open mind, and decide its time to look about. I brush my teeth and sling on some smelly stuff, but I don't bother to shave. I want to remain apart from the crowd of hip and clean looking dudes that inhabit the place. So far I have seen many perfectly manicured, groovy hair-styled, manufactured looking, young, trendy, touristic fashionistas. It seems to abound here, from what I can tell. I am a bum, not a kite-surfing 'pirate', sorry. It could very nearly be time to get drunk and verbally abuse some people. I am feeling a bit that way, it seems.

I leave my den carrying only my guitar and wander out then down the street towards the city centre. I enter it through an archway that heads down to the port. It's thin, white walls on both sides of me, and after entering the archway I look back. It might have once been a battlement gate or the outskirts of the city centre or something. The shops are very different in this part to what I have seen elsewhere. Most seem to be owned by white Europeans, and they all sell ethnic

Is this really who I am now?

stuff and are Moroccan themed on the inside. It's actually kind of trashy somehow, but certainly nothing is sold cheap. There is a dread-lock busker playing on the steps by the arch, I smile at him from safely behind my shades. He just looks away and continues. I stand to listen awhile. White-skinned dread-lock types. I lived through years of their pretentious bollocks in Oxford, and I don't much care for it. It often comes with that dog-on-a-rope style and dressage, anti-fashion is still a fashion. They are always such aloof bastards too. Special. The sound of his guitar resonates with a sweet reverberation off the tall walls in the thin white alleys. I notice we are alone. I feel in the kind of mood where I end up in fights, and then wonder why they started it. I guess I am not very happy here yet. I need to keep a check on that attitude. I would have liked to have kicked his ass though, it was just something in the look he gave me.

Further down and around the corner there are more shops and bars, all of which seem to be run by white, groovy, pseudo-ethnic types. This place is way too cool for me. In fact I think I am really starting to hate it here. This starts that bizarre internal argument - *maybe I hate them because I am just like them...maybe I have that same self-righteous certainty that I know best, and that everyone else is out of touch* - whatever. Stop it. Ssh!

A little further down, I round the port and spot what I guess must be the old castle. And then there it is, the sea to the south, the gateway beyond Europe. I look out over it and feel a certain satisfaction in doing so. Through the mist I can make out some dark hills and realise it might well be Africa. I have done what I came here to do. I have found the southern most point. From here on, it will be a return journey.

Women are actually prettier here than I at first gave the place credit for. I found the plaza strip that runs up from the port, and I sit outside for a cerveza. Still cloudy, but they are high clouds, and it shouldn't rain any time soon. The town is more awake now that it has gone 5 pm. A gorgeous, blond French woman sits nearby with her man, but it doesn't stop her looking over. She has that look. Cheeky but alert, and she reminds me of a young fairy godmother, but her

The Road to El Palmar

mannerisms smack of wealth and, dare I say, selfishness. She looks away each time that her fella catches her looking my way. Never trust a woman like that. I try to catch his eye to smile at him, let him relax, tell him I am okay and not a threat. *I get it mate, she is a total bitch, and you are stuck with her, unlucky.* But when he finally looks at me it is with a glare of hatred, so I drop my gaze and continue to write. Leave them to their demons, I have my own to contend with, thanks.

There is a much larger Guardia Civil presence on the streets here, and they are dog-ugly and pretty mean looking. I see one official car driven by what looks like a Rottweiler. Certainly hope to avoid them on this, my merry saunter around the town. The temperature drops a degree or two quickly, and I fear rain may be threatening a return after all. I don't think that I will busk here. Tarifa is not what I was expecting. If rains come tonight the streets will be empty anyway. I decide to return and start a pub-crawl of the bars that I saw.

I head down to the dock corner and position myself on a wall with the Mediterranean on one side and the Atlantic on the other. If I see one more goddamn tie-dye wearing hippy, I am going back to the hostel. This place is chock full of this faux-ethnic thing. It's feels pretty fake here. I didn't understand it back in Oxford in the eighties, and I don't get it now. I move on and find Café Central, near what seems like church gates. I sit to drink some more. It's busier here and holds a better vibrancy, more up-tempo. Music is playing that isn't ethnic but rather a cheesy euro-trash. A nice respite, surprisingly. There are three large and bald British hooligans drinking here not far away from me. My other least favourite type of creature is the football hooligan, having spent too many nights out in Watford and other football towns. I have no love of the British football thug mindset. I am actually feeling very bored here. Tarifa is culturally skint, a bit fake, fashionably run by pseudo-ethnic aloof wannabes, and seems to have been rebuilt by unskilled and possibly blind desperadoes, it's undeserving of anything that Paolo Coelho ever mentioned about the place. Where the hell did he stay? Must have been another Tarifa.

A blond woman shakes her hair at me. Probably the best piece of ass I have seen since I got here and my mind drifts to women again. This is the first town that I have not seen a 'club' in. Saw a few on the

Is this really who I am now?

bus journey here too. Grand haciendas, fantastic looking places. I would love to visit one, but have not enough money for it. Nor do I have the desire to break the bond of fidelity with my beloved girlfriend back home, of course. This is actually true, despite my roving eye and telling you all about it. You should probably know that she will no doubt read this anyway, when I accidentally leave this journal out and lying around one day. But I don't really hide my behaviours, though neither do I act on them very much. Am I making excuses? Maybe, or just being honest about my thoughts. Something about Tarifa makes me want to fight and fuck, possibly just out of boredom and frustration at the lack of connection with anyone. Funnily enough Watford does the same. If I fall foul of either one, I will try to make it the lesser of those two weevils, but I will do my best to avoid both. I don't really much feel like talking to people here, I am just wandering about and feeling a bit lost and out of place. I don't feel like I belong here. I also seem to have developed a bout of sarcastic venom, as can be measured by my writing no doubt, and that venom has often landed me in scrapes.

So after a brief bit of personal consultation and a stern pep-talk, I decide to chill the fuck out and find somewhere to sit this venomous period out. I feel like a wild animal that has accidentally stumbled into a city and become fearfully lost and a bit bitey. I wonder what happened to the spiritual journey I was on? Of course, I just never know when an angel will pop up and save me, so I don't give up hope yet. Must keep myself available, while trying to avoid the rut of cynical annoyance and aggressive behaviour. I am feeling a bit ship-wrecked here amongst these phantoms. What am I doing here in this pseudo-ethnic town with a peppering of white hooligan? I blame Paolo Coelho. He glammed the whole place up, the lying bastard. I should have known when I read a couple of his other books that he could not be trusted. He just wrote chick catnip, the tart.

I finally spot a few surfers and am glad to see them. Maybe there is some hope for the place yet. Surfers also tend to be stand-offish, but I would take them any day over what is currently around here. They are out for a laugh with less attitude, maybe the sea has groomed this healthier state of mind, the Landlord has grinned at them from inside the power of the wave. If you can amuse them with some bravado, you can usually get them on side. Not like morose, dread-locked, faux-ethnic dope heads, and these somewhat aloof and *aren't-I-so-god-damned-beautiful-but-don't-look-at-me* women. Tie-dye hippies too. I spit them. And the peppering of bald hooligans? Well they are just there to add to the glorious texture that is Tarifa tourism, I guess. What are they doing here?

I feel that glaze of an obnoxious sheen dropping down over my eyes as my fourth, or is it fifth, cerveza hits home. A couple of locals walking by give me the eyeball, then one asks me for a light. Sure, I can do that. I feel distressed and agitated, and I am being aggressive and feisty, which will for sure create trouble if I am not watchful of myself. I need something to do. I ponder the quandary. What to do tonight? Maybe some heavy drinking, some dark sarcastic humour, and forcing my way into other people's circles is on the menu. If I don't fall over drunk first, which right now is the most likely result, so maybe it is time to eat again.

I find a healthy looking food place on the road that leads down to the port from Café Central. It's small, but cosy, and will do for some eats. It's lined with bookshelves, all English books I note, must be all the bored travellers that end up in here and leave them behind. I see faces in here that I have seen already about town, Tarifa must be as small as it seems. I wait to get served, and then take a seat. Not long after get tired writing in cramped conditions, the place is pretty small and it has filled up a bit. Since everyone is English, and most of them can see my writing - it really is that small in here - I realise that I may have far too many 'fuck' words on my page. I ought to attempt actual communication anyway, so I put the book down.

As I relax into a few more cerveza, I feel quietly content to just sit and observe. Staying still is a smart move, and hiding out for a while in this cafe was too. I start to feel less anger, less rage, something was spinning me out of control, and it has been getting at me since I arrived. I guess it is just the annoyance at leaving the feeling of flow behind, finding it replaced by the mood of this town. I am not sure I like Tarifa all that much yet.

Is this really who I am now?

I spot orange trees with ripe fruit outside Café Zumo. I have lost the art of being charming and attractive to people, but seem to have improved my skills greatly in being a drunken and moody grouch, and I have never been far away from a fight when like this. It's a shame really, but I think that there is nothing I can do to immediately resolve the situation, so instead of losing myself in regrets of my life gone by, I resolve to try to drink myself through to the other side of it. There is no other recourse for a man of my years. I really have no idea how best to behave now that I approach forty, and I find my smile and any glint in the eye that I might once have had, has certainly begun to fade. It's a tough call to get used to, having the vigour and rigour start seeping away to a lost youth. Age does us no favours. I wake each morning to a greyer haired, more bamboozled looking creature staring back at me from the mirror. I look worn and tired. I admit it. I have to find a way to transcend the fickle life of a once lucky man and figure out how to grow old gracefully, or do I mean disgracefully? No. Definitely must leave the flirting and any hope of being a sexual conquistador behind me. It's not easy to let everything go, but I owe it to myself to find a way. Develop a detached but happy air, and instead of trying to enter every woman I see, just be nice to them instead. It isn't so hard to do, so I am told. Otherwise, there just comes a point when you are left howling like a wolf, dying lonely in the hills, probably lost in some foreign land, and no one will really much care at all and why would they? So, just relax you bastard! Relax, and maybe smile a bit. Stop trying to pick fights. Be nice. Leave that other game for the youth, it is more suitable for them now anyway. Changes in life, they really are a bitch. I think I am just feeling lonely, now that I am back amongst people.

As I set out to leave the cafe, two girls from Madrid stop me and, seeing my guitar, ask for a tune. Without hesitation I agree. I like this newfound willingness in me to play. I sit down next to the one called Bella and give her a song. She loves it. Half way through, a German girl comes out and sits down with us and seems happy to listen too. I finish up being Romeo, and then life returns to normal. We all talk a while, but in talking they seem less enthralled now. Something just isn't

The Road to El Palmar

working for me here. I am eager to keep the moment alive, so play another tune, but Bella now seems not sure what to do with herself, and that makes me uncomfortable, so I bring it to an early finish. The moment has become lost, as moments tend to do. Though truth be told, I am not sure the moment was really ever there at all. To exorcise the growing sense of awkwardness, I ask her where the better bars are and then everyone gets involved in the conversation and we all start to feel okay again. *Phew!* Bar Tomadido and Bar Sol are good, she tells me. I stay only long enough to be polite, and then take my leave. Not really sure what happened then, it went from warm to frosty quite suddenly, and I did not pick up on how or why. I thought maybe it was the playing, or maybe it was me talking. Maybe she could smell me. Who knows. Oh well.

I walk on up towards the arch where I entered in, and then wander about the central roads, ducking down a small side-street I find myself in what seems to be more like the real heart of Tarifa. It's the thing about coming to a new town, you have to walk through its useless, dead, inhospitable places first, often wondering what the hell you are doing there. As a result, at first, you may hate a place. But if you can give it time, try not to lose your noodle, and just keep open to opportunity, then you eventually ask enough people and you find the right information. Then maybe, if you are lucky, you find a good bar with *your* kind of people. The next thing you know you are having the time of your life. One wrong turn, and you can miss out on an entire life episode by just going home, it's that simple. This is the nature of travel in this way. It's a learnt skill, without a doubt.

I enter bar Tomadido, and instantly warm to it. I meet Bill W, he was on the bus with me but we didn't speak back then. He's old, bald and extremely slow and detached, but he buys me a drink all the same. I suspect he is a little bit queer judging from his somewhat pained ways and mannerisms. But a lovely guy all the same, and he soon leaves to go on a date with an 80 year old lady who runs a restaurant in Tarifa. She is a war veteran, by all accounts. He tells me that she used to fight for the Greek resistance. We toast an end to all wars, and then off he goes.

I then get chatting to Mauricio, the young Spaniard who runs the

Is this really who I am now?

bar. He's well travelled, good looking, and seems pretty straight up and genuine. He is happy to talk and serve at the same time. I stop to write this, and then continue chatting with some more people who have just come in. I am suddenly the busiest man in town. I feel like extending my journey into Morocco after talking to Mauricio and Bill.

Bill lives out there with his 'girlfriend', who is from Essex. I couldn't make him out in the short time that he lingered. He seemed unhappy and kind of locked down, but chatted animatedly if I spoke to him, though it felt like I had to keep leading it. It was like his mind was elsewhere, running at a different speed, because as soon as I decided that he really wasn't listening at all and turned away to look about for someone else to talk to, he sidled closer and then revealed something else. I liked him though. He was bordering on ancient, and those old-timers are always worth a listen. They've seen everything since the Second World War. Very different times to now, and they all have a story if you can coax it from them, though usually the problem is getting them to shut up once you do.

It's gone quiet again. The bar is in a moment of hush. Funny how that happens sometimes amongst groups of unconnected people. I notice that Absinthe is for sale from some chalk scratchings on a wall, gives me a shudder to recall a few shocking nights on that stuff. Mauricio points out a picture on another wall to me. It is an A0 size poster of two guys, a singer and guitarist. The singer looks a bit like Steve Tyler in a suit, and the guitarist, who looks adoringly at the singer, is the spitting image of the leader out of the band in the film *Rock Star* with Jennifer Anniston. Fuck. Why did I have to think of her now? That just reminds me of my girlfriend. Suddenly, I miss my girlfriend.

A giant man enters the bar and gives me a deep hello. He is English, armed with a Rottweiler in tow but it's cuddly, and so is he. Mauricio offers me the menu. I choose Octopus tapas. It's served quite quickly, is small and though tasty, doesn't really satisfy. So I follow it with a large tuna and mozzarella sarnie, and now I feel fed. I realise Mauricio is Italian, not Spanish as I first thought, I find this out when the bar is invaded by his nationals. They are likable, but loud and speak too quickly, like most Italians when they are in groups. I am not sure I

The Road to El Palmar

can be done with the overly energetic vibe that is now developing, and so I give Mauricio a wave of thanks and then leg it. When the Italians came in, the music got turned up louder. Too much staring into space while listening to boom-boom dance music does me no good these days.

I wander back through deserted streets. It is now 11 pm. It's my nature to seek pleasure, and right now, on a lonesome night in Tarifa before the summer season starts, I am trying to think what to do next for kicks. I find Bar Sol that Bella had talked about and realise it is in fact called Bar Soul and it opens at 11 pm. I try the door. It is closed. I look again at the sign. Opens at 11 pm... but not on Mondays. Which is probably a good thing, because I then head back to my hostel, lay down on my bed and reflect on the night.

Put me in the surrounds of El Palmar and I find my spiritual side, put me in a place like Tarifa, and I turn into a drink fuelled Lothario who is liable to get a bit scrappy and eventually send things south. I don't really like Tarifa, though I feel unfair in saying it, but I feel that I have out-grown places like it. I only discover this fact by coming here alone and by having the time and space to consider it. I think that I am over this way of life in general. The booze, the drugs, the chasing of intoxicated fun through night time bars and clubs, and the whole party thing. I am just getting too old for it. My girlfriend and friends would love it here, I suspect, which also kind of worries me. I can't seem to quite figure out how to retire gracefully from places like this. It feels like the old *me*, and that I need to figure out how to leave this side of myself behind. But I can't figure out how to come to places like this and not end up drunk in bars, staring into space, talking to other drinkers, flirting with women, and then thinking about what mischief I can get up to. It is, after all, what I have always done in the past. I don't suppose it matters much to be this way, but somehow I am tired of it. You go where you go, and you do what you do, and you do it in the way that you do it. If that makes any kind of sense. But if in your heart of hearts, when you get back to whatever place that night is called home, you don't really rate whatever it was that you found out there and went along with it just because you had nothing better to do, then maybe it is time to bugger-off, and don't return without good

Is this really who I am now?

reason or persuasion to do so. Tarifa, I just don't think you and me are going to be good friends somehow.

Cars whistle by outside, and in my drunken end-of-holiday stupor, I am tempted to go find a taxi and demand to be taken to the best 'club' in town. I am intrigued, having seen so many. But it will cost me money that I don't want to spend, and I will end up truly worn out and totally legless, and though probably vaguely amused, I will also in the end feel completely dissatisfied and spiritually empty. Then, I will come home at about 5 am to catch a tired bus at 10:30 am. I will sleep off-and-on until I get home to London, and that is just the logistics, the emotional trauma that I will likely feel for being such a scum-pup, that, will never wear off. It is not that I don't love prostitution, I do. It is the fact that I am mostly betrothed, and she is a good person, and I am probably not, but I do try. So instead of heading out whoring, I call it a day, and bed down in the 15-euro hostel with a flashing hallway light and two hot taps but no bathroom, to ponder on the strange paradox that I find myself in. I appear to be torn between the love of vice and an impossible dream of escape. I expected more from Tarifa, but I am sure I got all that I deserved. I also smoked 20 Chesterfields today, and that was just since 5 pm. Is this really who I am now?

A change of perception

I awoke at 5 am after some heavy-duty dreaming, most of which escapes me now. I recall it ending with a little dark-haired girl staring at me from beside the bed. She seemed like a ghost, and I woke up half expecting to see her standing there. I got up and had a smoke to calm down and then fell back to sleep, awaking next at 7 am.

I lay there wondering about how much the mood of travel had changed since leaving El Palmar, or rather since arriving in Tarifa. Tarifa seemed to hold no secrets for me. I guess the only real character of depth I met here was Bill. Other than that, I seemed to find nothing much of value. I don't think my coming here was a mistake, but it just seems to be a bit empty of anything. I wonder if the sense of being at one with my life and having direction, that intensity, was something to do with El Palmar, or maybe it came from living rough on the beach beside the sea. In this rented room, my senses and thoughts are returned to all things normal. There are no stars overhead at night, no waves lapping on nearby sands, just cars and the incessant noise of people. Maybe it is time for me to leave these urban dwellings and seek nature, seek places where nature can be seen and heard, and where it can break through. What is natural in a town after all? Everything gets concreted over.

I am glad that I hunted further through the streets of Tarifa last night, eventually coming to what seemed like its heart. In the end I found some great shops, restaurants and bars too, and it changed my initial perspective on the place. It does indeed have a charm of it's own, and I will leave here liking it and with pleasant enough memories. Tarifa, I apologise for being rude about you at first, it was definitely me and not you.

The day begins with hints of clouds, uncertain whether to clear or to build into rain, but who cares when it's warm. I head for Jerez de la Frontera today, the inland town. Famous for its sherry, horses, and of course flamenco. I had hoped to find out more on this trip about those

A change of perception

purveyors of violence and robbery, murderers of indigenous, and borrowers of their gold, those infamous brigands the Conquistadors. Haven't seen a thing about them at all. I am also slightly surprised that I saw no Mayan features in any faces here on the south-west coast of Spain. In fact that is wrong, one lad in El Palmar had that distinctive Mayan profile but other than that, nothing. Here in Tarifa I was expecting to find the hordes of Islam, dens full of hookahs, night markets and casbah's, smoking genies and men in turbans trying to sell me magic carpets. Tarifa is certainly totally devoid of all that from what I can tell. Instead it appears to be run by white, middle-class, pseudo-ethnics. I only saw two non-white people the entire time. To me that makes it a soulless caricature of what it once was, or maybe wasn't, it is hard to tell. At least there are no fish-and-chip shops here. It is half-past eight, and time to go in search of breakfast. I may as well check-out of here now too.

My body is dreading having to put on the rucksack. I struggle painfully down the road, knots forming nicely in my shoulders after yesterday. I fight the urge to drop it. I breathe in, hoping oxygen might convince my body to work. I don't like the stigma of walking around with a guitar and a rucksack. People are not unfriendly, but I am aware that I am looking like a traveller, and there are times I don't want to stand out in quite that kind of a way. I certainly wont be getting dreadlocks, not deliberately anyway.

I must remember to find a room with a shower facility tonight in Jerez. My hair is still matted with salt and sand, and though I wont have time to wash my clothes, at least I could feel a little cleaner beneath them. My T-shirt now virtually un-wearable. There is something quite satisfying about being this unkempt and de-sanitised, forget fashionable changes of attire to match every occasion, just wear the same damn clothes every day. Why not? Many people fear not washing, my skin actually feels better for it, but then I do have psoriasis and maybe that is part of my pleasure at being this way. I try to get plenty of olive oil and tomatoes into me on holidays, especially if it's going to be spent in the sun. I am after some tomatoes now, but don't find them in the cafe I have entered, so I settle for a cooked breakfast instead and, of course, lots of *cafe con leche*. I think I could possibly live without booze or food, so long as I had cigarettes and coffee. It is now time for some philosophical breakfast musing.

Nature will outlast humanity. Despite all the concrete and cities that man builds, as soon as man leaves them, Nature will return and break through. It will grow between the cracks in the walls, and will gradually break open the tarmac too, until eventually it takes back the land again. Nature is wild at her core, but something in man fights against that. We can't stop our desire to progress because it is something written into our design, but we can't eradicate the innate force of Nature either. In the end it will be here long after we are gone. We spring from her, so even if somehow we beat her, we still lose. What exactly is Nature? The very driving force of life itself, maybe. Is it *of* the earth, is it *in* the earth, or *from* the earth, who knows? Is Nature anywhere else in the cosmos other than here? We do not know. What is it? This we do not really know either. Lots of questions, not many answers.

I often wondered about the various paradoxes that exist between Mankind and Nature. Man is wholly a part of Nature, we spring from her bosom and then in using the very power she gives us, we strive to defy her. We design the un-natural. Immortal plastic, for instance. Why would something springing from Nature then try so hard to disassociate itself from her? And even more curious, is that Nature herself should design and encourage her offspring to do it. We have run amok here in her sandpit, but she made us this way, she is responsible for us and our capabilities. Strange as it may seem, for us to do these things then Nature must be working through us. Therefore, everything we do, everything we make, everything we achieve, is still at some level, Nature. Be it immortal plastic, concrete, or even the atomic bomb, it's being made by Nature through Man. Man also appears to be struggling to achieve immortality for himself, struggling to figure out how to refuse Nature's call to die, while at the same time creating brilliant ways in which to go extinct quite quickly. Man is seemingly at war with Nature. We fear Nature, as much as we cannot live without her.

A change of perception

But something is missing from this jigsaw puzzle. Something does not add up about this fight. Why on earth would we do such a thing? What possible benefit do we gain by fighting the one thing we cannot afford to become completely disconnected from? Maybe eventually, man will figure it out and start to get things right. Start to use his skills and capacity of design and manipulation, to progress and push himself towards some greater goal, and not just towards the lifeless, dark death, of a drip-fed, plastic-lined immortality. On the flip-side, he might just accidentally nuke himself, and then it wont much matter.

I guess in my own way, that is what I am out here to try to find an answer to - the purpose and meaning of my existence in Nature. I get it all wrong, just like we all do, but in looking around these towns and cities that I travel through, I am trying to find clues as to how to get it right. Trying to find a way out from what I see happening around me, and yet everywhere I go it is much the same. Maybe in some ways I am trying to wake up to my natural spirit once again. I wonder what it would mean if we actually could get back to what the African bushman of old had, our indigenous pagan ancestors had, the Mayans too maybe, or the Australian aborigines. Don't get me wrong, I don't buy into that story either. But there is a curious similarity between the indigenous peoples of all countries. They seemed to have very similar ways of behaviour before whatever evolution of the mind brought them the concepts of religion, civilisation, progress, possession and ownership. The world is now set up to stop you returning to that indigenous way of life. You simply can't give up your personal possessions and enter into a life of spiritual oneness with Nature anymore. People have tried, and failed. The idea of living in mud-huts and living off the land is not as romantic as it might seem to some. I am certainly not deluded by this romantic ideal at all, but there is something that exists in the mindset of the indigenous human of yore that differs greatly from that of our mindset - the one required for living in modernity today. Things have changed, and it is likely of little value to attempt to go back. For starters you will be trespassing on someone else's piece of land if you tried. But there is an issue with ownership too, because any land you own, really is not your own, it could easily be taken back by the Government in a coup, or simply

The Road to El Palmar

built over by a freeway in the name of progress. Property is mostly theft and always was. The Church, or a King, bashed someone on the head and stole it in the first place. That is the history of most land ownership if you care to look back far enough.

Buying land. It is not an answer. There is no sense of security in that act either, despite what people think. I know this because my mortgage terrifies me, and I don't like having it. I don't feel safe in it, it feels more like a weight by which to sink me. But there is no way back to an indigenous style of living. No way to live off the land, it just doesn't work anymore, mostly because population numbers are now so large that there is not room for us all if we did. But going forward, there is no great future in sight either. Over-population and lack of resources will, at some point, become much bigger issues here.

My hunch is that there is something at work in all this that we have failed to identify, something involved in driving our human desire for progress. Something possibly quite nefarious and that does not have humanities best interests at heart. There seems to be something forcing our mindset down pathways that are simply not good for our species in the long-term. Or maybe we are on the right track just making mistakes as we go, and eventually we will figure it out just fine, and there will be a bright future that everyone can agree on.

Meantime, how do you resolve the paradox? Man versus Nature and the pointlessness of such a battle. I have no idea. Strapped in as I am to a mortgage for decades, with other debts for at least the next few years. Living my life, doing a job I don't feel is really me, with barely any time to do what I feel really *is* me. Shit, I don't know what being *really me* even means. Who does?

Somehow, from within our enslavement to modernity, we have to find a deeper sense of purpose and meaning. Maybe if we could collectively let go of the urge to 'own' and 'possess', that might be something, but is such a change even possible? I doubt it. Now our trajectory seems set, and that can be distinctly nihilistic looking at times, if we are honest about it. I took a lot of drugs looking for answers, but it turned out that drugs held no answers, and fighting the system has not ever produced a solution either, it just creates another system, and it is never any better. The revolution goes in circles. It's as

A change of perception

if humanity is doomed to spin in circles, forever chasing his tail, rather than finding a way to evolve out of the crises of energy, resources, war, and population-overload that we are inevitably bound towards. Hell, maybe there are no answers.

Along the way I came across things like meditation, enlightenment, detachment, Buddhism... and I realised that there may actually be something of promise in following those pathways. Rather than trying to fix anything, it is about letting go of our attachment to outcomes. Letting go of the urge to force a change upon the universe outside of us, and instead look within. Change, they say, is only possible within.

So, is meditation the way out of this apocalyptic end-game being faced by modernity? Maybe it is not so much a *way out*, as a way of letting go of our concern about it. In the process seeing a bigger picture - our journey through this life flowing ever on into a timeless eternity. Maybe the only change possible, is the change that we can make in ourselves. And that will only ever be a change made in our perception.

I look up and out of the door of the cafe where I am sitting this morning. There I see a palm tree set amongst a backdrop of marble, metal, concrete, glass, and petroleum-burning traffic. Beneath it all, beneath this cafe, and the machinery, and the concrete, and the city itself, the whole earth thrums alive with the forces of Nature. This is just the surface - an ugly and shallow paint job, a realm of electro-mechanical static. A veneer designed to hold back Nature and that allows us to ferry to and fro safely above her, while at the same time squander every energy resource we can find. All the while beneath us lurks that immense, infinite, and unstoppable power. One that has been here much longer than we have, and is probably not at all threatened by our mistakes.

I let my eyes go into a soft focus, and I imagine that I am looking through the ugliness of this concrete wasteland, down into the heart of Nature herself. It has a strange, dislocating effect upon me to do so. Immediately revealing to me that this dirty town, a city of electricity, engines and clutter, is only a temporary thing, and actually it struggles to run. This human ant-hill is inconsequential in the grand scheme of things. It would be obvious, if I was not so obsessed with feeling resentment of some kind towards my own-kind for our current state of existence. But something else did this to us, I feel certain of it. We have been diverted from a much better way by something that has not been good for us, but has turned us into blind, homicidal amnesiacs. I let my focus, my awareness expand. I try to connect with Nature and feel into the eternity that exists in the future, far beyond her time too. What will be here in the cosmos when Nature is gone? It is just like when I focused beyond my death that day at the beach, doing this exercise brings me an unexpected feeling of peace. Where moments before I felt singed, scorched, and empty, now I feel calmer. Just by shifting my focus it no longer seems so important at all that humanity, or Nature, might be doomed. When it is all done and dusted, when it is all gone, then how much will this moment really matter anyway?

I open my eyes again. I look around the cafe at the people here. It's in their eyes too. Nature is somewhere deep inside every one of us. Hidden, suppressed maybe, but every single living being goes right to the source. All the way down there to the heart of Nature. Every single beautiful one of us. Maybe none of this matters at all. Maybe I am concerning myself with all the wrong things because I feel trapped by my own life choices right now.

I feel like I have tapped into another secret today. The Earth. Nature. Nothingness. The time beyond it all. And what are we exactly? What are we even doing here in this hallucination? All of us, at once capable of the deepest and most sincere form of love, that can switch in the blink of an eye to the most savage form of barbarism, and it often does. We are Nature at her finest. Brutal, murderous, glorious, and given to bloodshed and carnage in the extreme. She truly is the most fantastic serial killer, and often uses us to do her bidding. That's what it means to be human. We are Gods and we are Devils, we are Apex predators, destroyers and unique designers of the world about us, and yet we remain completely enslaved to her. I suspect Nature is far more in charge of all this than we think.

I now feel like my head is going to explode if I keep this up. So I stop writing and finish off my breakfast. Then I read an English newspaper for a while to bring things back down to where we are all

A change of perception

sitting. I finish another coffee, and then a little while later, I leave.

Tarifa seems quite small, socially speaking. As I wait here for the bus, I am seeing all the same faces that I did yesterday. It's a community and probably a good one, but not one I found much to resonate with. Maybe I just did not give it long enough. There goes Bill again, a subtle acknowledgement we give each other. I find myself wondering again about what I am really doing out here. Where am I headed in my life? What is it that I seem to be looking for and have triggered in myself by coming out here? It is like I am looking for a tribe, a place to belong and feel welcome, and yet I have my own people back home waiting for me to return.

And now I have that strange anxiety invading my system again as I write these things, as if some great sin is committed by my daring to entertain leaving my life and making a huge change, something that I admit I am being tempted to do. It is going to be no easy journey to return home now. Something has woken up in me out here, something I cannot quite figure out, but neither can I put it back now that it has been unleashed. I feel like I am about to make a run across no-mans land, but with no real certainty of what lies on the other side. I finally made it to Tarifa and now, surprisingly quickly, I have decided to leave it again. Jerez my final stop before heading home.

The history of atoms

On the bus we pass back through the lands of green. Huge white stalks nesting on tall pylons, maybe ten of them. The biggest damn birds I have ever seen, and they all sit motionless and just stare at each other, a-buzz with stork communication. Weird. Like how horses stand dead still and yet seem to be in communion. Those stalks must be five feet tall, incredible things.

We passed the turning to El Palmar again, headed North to Jerez this time. A cloud in the sky shaped like smoke from a cannon-blast jogs my recollection. I remember now, I dreamed of galleons fighting and cannons firing in the night. I dreamed of Trafalgar, bloody death, guns, carnage, and war. And now I pass by the tower, below which I slept the night that I left El Palmar. Looking out to sea at the very spot that the battle drifted to. Blood in the water, bodies and wood all washing up on the beach. Did I die there in another incarnation? Was I swallowed up by the ocean in a little piece of history back in 1805? Sometimes I wonder on such things. It is as if I know the feeling of war at sea, as if it is a memory that I can't quite wake to. I have dreamed of it before. The dark ocean holds a terror, it scares me to gaze into it, at the same time it is impossible to go further into that feeling in order to know what exactly it is. I have tried. Is this all some regurgitation of a memory, a forgotten life gone by? Maybe someone else's life? The bits of us that float around the universe and always have, memories stored in hydrogen atoms, is that possible? Always changing and moving on through different forms. Every atom in us has been here since the beginning of time. What stories would they tell us, if we could tap into them. It would for sure be terrifying. One life is challenging enough to face up to, the last thing one needs to be consumed by is the experiences of other lives and their births and endings. Energy is constantly changing form, it is never destroyed. Energy in motion, e-motion, carried in atoms moving on through history without end. Was I a Spaniard maybe, ship's cook and

The history of atoms

concubine sunk on a vessel somewhere out there? Did great white sharks tear at my dying flesh? Or maybe I just sank without trace into the depths. Born again in another time with an acute case of Thalassophobia and Selachophobia. Or maybe parts of my body washed up on the shore at that very spot where hundreds of years later I am drawn to set up a tent, to muse and to ponder my inconsequential existence, and to wonder why I feel anxious and strange.

I can almost believe it, and maybe that is why it was here at El Palmar where things felt like they awaited my return. My ability to find my way here might well have now triggered something bigger in my life. Set something else in motion. Maybe a new phase, a new chapter in my journey, or maybe nothing much at all. This place, could it have meant something to me in another life, another time? Are these things even possible? If not *my* life, then maybe just the energetic imprint of someone else's who happened to have my atoms in them at the time. They now reside within me because I ate a chicken, that ate a plant, that grew from the earth, that had been shat on by a bird, that ate a seed, that fell from a flower, that grew on a beach, where hundreds of years before some deck-hand washed up on the beach dead, his blood sunk down into the sand until later it became food for the plant that grew. It is actually not so strange a connection to make through time if we follow the history of the atoms.

And so too maybe Karma, and energy, and the unfinished businesses of our lives that also get carried through the eternity of time by those same atoms that make up the bodies of the physical world. What if atoms can also carry an energetic imprint of our emotional responses at the time? The unfinished acts, begun in each one of those lives and the emotional accounts often left unclosed. Where do those things go if energy cannot be destroyed, but can only ever change form?

An African elder told me about that, and told me indigenous cultures had known this all a long. Debt's always had to be paid, and if they were not, then they would find a way to follow a lineage through time.

I feel strange now thinking about it all. Slightly mad. Going madder. I shut my eyes. Meditate for a bit. Calm. Soon the madness eases. I smile, and look out of the window. Spain going by. The 21st Century going by. My life-story going by. And all we can ever really try to do is try to enjoy the journey. As Pangloss said in Candide's Voltaire, *all is for the best, in the best of all possible worlds.*

City of wild Spanish horses

I like Jerez from the off, though I don't really know quite why. As I walk through its centre the shops are tacky and there is a hubbub of people. The streets and walls are dirty and wider than the towns I have been in so far. It is as you would expect of a big city, and yet I feel at ease and welcome. I feel anonymous too. The dark-haired, strong and elegant looking Spanish ladies are in force here. I find myself at one point coughing and spluttering and it turns out that quite by accident it was a startlingly good impression of a horse. The spirit of Jerez and its horses. Time to trot on and search out a map, and then a place to stay.

I find both pretty easily, and seeing how I am already in a good and central part of the town, I grab the first half decent looking hostel for a fair price, it is 21 euros. It has a nice picture of a Spanish flamenco dancer in the room, and better than that, it has a bath and shower. *Hallelujah!* This pleasure I will save for tomorrow, or maybe even tonight. I want to enjoy my outcast state a little bit longer. So I head back to the streets with my guitar.

While walking around in the afternoon sunshine, I spot two women sat at a cafe with rucksacks. I say *Ola*, and soon find out they are German and that they are friendly. They tell me that they are headed to Malaga and the South coast. I don't ruin their expectations by telling them how it isn't a touch on the south-west coast of Spain, at least in my opinion. One of them begins to show me on her map where their youth hostel is. As she does so, the soft hair of her arm rubs against mine and she lingers there. I am overcome with sensual pleasure, the electricity of connection rushing through me and I look up and into her eyes. She smiles at me, and then continues talking. She does not pull away. I can't break my attention away from the feeling. I am left uncertain what to say. I re-find my composure and we chat for a little while longer, and some time later I wish them luck on their trip, and depart.

I sit at an outside cafe and order up some seafood. a short time later my Paella arrives. I start to eat. Hot damn, it is way too hot. Okay, I write some more instead. I am thinking more on the experience I just had with a nameless Germanic female that I will never see again. What was that all about? It used to be that I would chase such things, but I have been in a steady relationship for a number of years now, and so those days are behind me. I do not chase such situations at all anymore, but then neither do they arise all that much. Most of the time I am out with my girlfriend, or amongst people who know me, and so little interaction of that nature takes place. I guess it was perfectly normal, I have just forgotten what it is like when a woman offers an invitation.

I finish eating and then wander for a while. Sitting in the almost empty park by Alecar, I think it is called that, and it has the most gorgeous pink, flowering trees. I play there for an hour or so, trying to dispel the anxiety attack that decided to creep up on me a little while ago. Always seems to be the same deal - anxiety in the end and sometimes so hard to dispel. An hour or so later it has lifted and I can move off, back to where I was in the busy city streets, I find a cafe toilet and in there I unleash like a Jerez pony.

Exiting the ablutions, I am accosted by a drunk who won't now leave me alone and keeps nagging me to play. I eventually give up trying to shake him, and honour his request, why not? *If you can walk with the crowd and keep your virtue, or walk with kings, nor lose the common touch... something, something, something... you'll be a man my son.* But as soon as I start up, the dimwit muscles in and tries to show me flamenco. He can't seem to figure out that I am a left-hander, and struggles to focus on my guitar as he sways back and forth in front of me. I wish he would not keep touching me nor my guitar. I feel like hitting him each time he does. Everyone has their limits and I am now getting pretty tired of him, but there is no easy shaking the freaks and the geeks. Sometimes, it is better to suffer the crazy, but he seems not to be tiring of annoying me yet. It is sunny still, and with him around, I don't feel like busking.

I sit down at a cafe that has chairs in the street, choosing a table with only one chair to see if that works to stop him loitering around me. It is still busy round here, and I watch the people to-ing and fro-

City of wild Spanish horses

ing. The guy is not deterred and remains hovering like a confused vulture, swaying dangerously but somehow managing not to fall down. I finally tell him that he needs to fuck off. He knows exactly what I am saying, but ignores it like a professional. Then some time later, and quite unexpectedly, and long after I have given up trying to shake him, he just ups and leaves. I had struggled with his drunken and intrusive touching and his incessant attempts at hand-shaking, it was just too much. I don't go well with anyone being falsely friendly, especially when they are on the booze. It's actually quite useful having this notebook to hide in. *Ah.* I wrote too soon. He is back and trying to get my attention again. He's a bloody wasp. More beggars come by.

"No dinero...piss off!" I tell them.

Lots of Germans here. The haggard, old and arrogant kind. The women wearing floral patterns and gold chains. Some of them pay the beggars and make a point of wanting to be seen to do it. No doubt it feels good, no idea that they are helping no one and nothing, nought but the sham existence of us all. Creating an addiction to handouts, that is the sum total of charity giving. Money in exchange for some appeasement of their own guilt, no doubt. I still feel a touch odd. Not down, nor up, just odd.

Oh my. Now some quite trashy looking girls sit down near me. All lipstick and *ass-and-tits-tight* clothing. I kind of like the trashy girls. What is going on in me, I can't relax and can't shake this odd feeling. *Pleasure you can't measure, and pain you can't explain.* This is the no-mans land between moments.

A hippy girl with dreadlocks is busking over yonder. Remember this, it is the golden rule of busking, never play within a thousand yards of lady buskers, they always get the money. She's another one that is begging though, not busking at all. Plays her recorder for one second, and then bounces round the street accosting people, giving them smiles as she blocks their way, batting her eyelids and then reacting with scornful looks if they turn her down. I think she just spat on that man when he turned his back to her. The entitlement is strong in that one. Her fella sits on the corner smoking roll-ups and looking shifty. If Bik was here he might call them *Parasitititites*. Though I dislike the bums that beg-not-busk, I have to admire the air of *I-don't-give-a-single-*

fuck that enables them to be that way. Not admire, actually that is the wrong word, maybe I am mildly envious at some level. I don't want to feel like a sham myself. Yet are we not all just bums? It is so confusing.

My mood is not the best right now. How can I turn it around and into something more positive? I need to energise, this has held me in its spell too long. Singing and writing don't cure it today. I wonder what would, other than another course of medicinal alcohol abuse. Jesus, I probably am an alcoholic, maybe that is the problem. Pretty obvious to a non-drinker, I suppose.

I try tensing all my body muscles, sometimes that works. Forcing the energy out from my middle somewhere. Breathe. *Just breathe in the air.* More beggars come by. This town is rich with poor people kow-towing to the rich for pieces of eight. I shake my legs, trying to hit upon a motion that might dispel the mood. The ache. The longing. The anxiety.

It is 5:30 pm and the streets are coming back to life again, they have been in a lull for an hour or two. Maybe after this cup of tea I should busk my sad blues away. Woo some ladies as they pass me by. There are many beauties here in this city of wild Spanish horses.

I stand in front of what I soon realise is a lingerie shop. I did not know this when I began singing. There's a row of mannequins watching me from the window and also three models watch down on me from street posters, like angels come to hear me, and I honour them by drifting away. I play to them for nearly two hours, and learn that busy commercial shopping streets do not make for good busking, not in my style anyway. I am gentle, soft-voiced, and need the reverberation of thin alleys, they seem to be my predilection. Like an alley cat, I imagine. The poor give, the rich pretend to, and I make two euros in the two hours that I play. The mannequins and poster models show more emotional reaction than most. I go through every song I ever wrote that was for the acoustic guitar. There are moments I feel stupid, and moments I feel as if the Spirit has descended upon me, almost feeling that I touch the heart of the matter. I love music when it feels good, feels like a channel to the divine. For the most part, playing in the city street is a cold experience, cold as in heartless rather than in

City of wild Spanish horses

temperature, but it is an experience all the same, and I'll take it.

I leave there at 7:30 pm feeling tired and hungry again. I take another wander. I catch the eye of a strange looking lady, she is pretty but old. She is wearing all white, and I think her to be a witch. I tell her so, but she doesn't understand English, and then tries to offer me jewellery that she has in a bag. I see she is some kind of street-seller. Our conversation is unable to go very far, it's a shame, I would have liked to have talked to her and found out what she was about. I bid a gentlemanly goodbye to her, and move on.

I find a nice plaza, it is busy with people just hanging about and it has a large tree dominating it. I stop there for a beer. The barman is slick and tough, but he is being quite funny and at some point comes over to my table and then introduces me to two young Spanish ladies who are on a table not far away. He is saying one is a genius at flamenco dance, and that I should play for her. I am pained again to decline, in this country of guitar skills that are so far above my lowly strumming, it isn't even worth being upset about it. I have to decline some further requests, sinking instead into happy comfort that beer on an empty stomach brings. Yes, definitely an alcoholic. I heard it makes the best writers. Makes them shoot their heads off in the end too. Happy daze. Here's to writer's who don't blow their brains out.

The flamenco woman leaves, and then I notice her friend who was obscured by her and who remains sat down. She reminds me of a girl I know at work. I recognise the same nature in her, it is like looking at a Spanish version. Beautiful, voluptuous, hints of warmth and friendliness, and a gift for talking incessantly. I laugh just watching her. She is talking to a girl friend sat with her. She wont look at me, however hard I try to get her attention.

If you lived in Spain and wanted to find love, then I have a hunch that there is no better place you could come to than Jerez. I can feel something here, waiting to be wooed, something almost traditional, something classy. It's in the eyes of the women. Tough, observant, critical, yet I sense they would be very capable of satisfying. I am attracted to what I see here. They might want kids, devotion, and a good life. Nothing wrong with that, I suppose. Given the way the place accepts the 'club' bordellos, I guess they might even allow their men a

The Road to El Palmar

little straying too, so long as it was not with his heart.

I meet my second beer and try to break my gaze from her gorgeous, big white front-teeth. Though my illusion is suddenly shattered when I realise that I have just heard her say *'puta'* at a girl that walked by. She is now the winning favourite. The best I have seen since being here in Spain, feisty, and I like that. I swear she's read me already, her evasion at my attempts in getting any eye-contact too perfect to sustain belief otherwise. People always want to know what is going on around them. The clue is in the opposite of what you expect them to do, especially where the female of the species is concerned.

I make for the toilets, and after having to get the lock picked by a local with a toothpick, I check my dressage and do a button or two up. Hairy chests loose in the courtyard, just wont do. A little while after my return she stands up preparing to leave, and finally her eyes look my way. We don't exchange smiles, just a look held for the briefest of moments. How many of these moments pass us by in life? Moments of connection. But we remain lost in our thoughts and doubts, uncertain whether to chase and try to make an opportunity, open up a door that might allow us to enter in. We can choose to act, or we just dither and then let it pass us by. There are so many doors of opportunity every day, that it is probably important to choose wisely, or we might find ourselves lost down roads that we never really wanted to travel and on which we might stay for entire lifetimes. Sometimes we should hold out and wait. Wait for that perfect opportunity, wait for wisdom and knowledge enough to know that when it comes, it is the right one. How many of us jump too soon, or fear acting when it finally shows up? Roads to nowhere. I am wise enough now. I don't want to give any more of myself away, or so I would like to believe. Then eventually, after years of playing the game you start to wonder if maybe you missed the best opportunities, or maybe you took them, how can you ever really know? She turns away, the moment is gone. I wont be chasing her, though I saw no sign of invite anyway. I just wanted to catch her eye, to see her.

The next busking session is much better and more relaxed. I start making stuff up, and find something fitting to sing about from the

City of wild Spanish horses

world going on around me. Jamming the tune as I go. I face the setting sun for a while as I play, and enjoy the warmth and the scenery from between two orange trees. This feels really good. Much better way of playing too, especially if not many people are paying attention. I am enjoying this method much more. I make about four more euros in just less than two hours of playing. I still assume they must think me a guitar retard. I also discover that you should not leave too much loose change on your bag that you lay out. Keep it at two coins of a high denomination, and you'll be fine. Not too much, and not too little. Actually I just remembered one of those coins I started with is mine, so that's three bucks made, not four. Hard crowd to please in Jerez. It's 9:30 pm now. Still light. I was playing one of my own songs about a tryst with three women. Just at that moment three girls went by, and one kept my gaze with a smile as she went past. It all felt a bit rock and roll for a moment.

"I do it for love!" I shouted after her.

I actually had no idea why that came out of my mouth. One of them came back and told me, apologetically, that she had no money. I told her it was fine, and that it wasn't the money that I did it for, but simply the love of music and of my guitar. It was cliched as hell but did actually have a ring of truth to it. They laughed and then waved at me and one blew a kiss and they all went on their way. That, I liked, and it made the entire effort of playing worthwhile.

I have now sat down at one of the three bars that were near me. All of them have outside areas. The other two bars are full, while mine is empty, except of course for me. I didn't pick it for that reason, or maybe I did, but did not realise it was what drew me to sit here. But now I am sat here it is a very strange sensation, I suddenly feel like a prostitute. I write in part to ignore the fact that I stand out sitting here on my own.

It definitely needs amplification, what I do. I do not play loudly and all my acoustic stuff works best with dynamics. That is something that gets completely lost when playing in a noisy street. A touch of reverb would help too, and something to project the whole thing, then I could ease back on my playing and work on the gentle notes, the emptiness between them. I stick to minor keys mainly. I like laments,

The Road to El Palmar

and heartfelt tunes. I may do one more night-time set before I turn in. The streets are quieter now, so I might try and find a nice alley with a touch of natural reverb for my plucky numbers. Leave the begging to the monkey character that I saw earlier. He was in shades, with a nylon guitar that he held up by his ear, a fat-assed wife in tow. He had a stupid tail-coat on and walked too quickly, with his torso leaning too far forward all the time. I saw him wander round the cafes hitting some notes, then turning his guitar bottom-side down and sticking it into the peoples faces who were sat down eating and drinking. Amazingly he does quite well hassling people like that, and though he probably means well, he is bit of a spiky weasel on the beg, not playing much at all. At least give them a tune, man, come on!

This place is dead now, just the feeders at the bars and cafes. City-sharks come in to feast at twilight. It is soon time to move onto the whisky and coke. I met another two buskers, the man and woman with an accordion that I saw early on in the day. Kept walking past my two coins and laughing at me. They were trying to psyche me out. Dirty world this busking business, it's dog eat dog. So I went and spoke to them when I next saw them. They told me they were from Romania, they didn't look like it to me. She looked Indian-American and he looked like a dodgy Greek, but who knows. Good luck to them. This is fun for me, for them it's probably survival.

I'm in the Dolce Vita. Cafe and *helandos*. I guess that means either prostitute or damn uncomfortable plastic chairs because that's all they have here right now. I wonder where the action is in this town at night. This zone died right as the sun went down. Better not get so drunk that I cant figure where my hostel is. I do feel a drinking session coming on though. It's my last night to make it count.

10:30 pm and the night is now officially dead here in Jerez. I hit the last bar that was still open. I try and order JD and coke but told they only have Balantine. It's posh in here, and they even bring the bottle to your table and then pour the whisky until you say stop. Which in my case was nearly to the top of a long glass, since I had no idea what the plan was. That's me done for then.

I wandered the night time streets after leaving the Dolce Vita, but

City of wild Spanish horses

cities are just too big; you could walk for days and still get nowhere. So I doubled back and returned to Bar Domecq. Quaint but...Shit! This Balantine is gonna kill me. The machine is out of smokes too, so I end up with Blue Fortune. Yea, feeling lucky. Sounds good, but sure to be deadly, just as the Balantine is fast proving to be. Holy cow. That is kicking my ass. What whisky wisdom will befall me this hour? I am beyond food now, but I will play for sex or money.

Two ladies, about my age, avoid my look. Hmm. I should probably mention - again - that I am *not* wolfing it up here in Spain. I am just interested to meet whoever I meet, nothing more. I swear. I don't know how one puts that across to people who assume all lone men to be...lone men... okay, fair point. I am still a Testosteronically fuelled pervert, that doesn't really ever change much. You got me there.

I like the way they make the bars in the streets of Jerez. Using old sherry kegs, the barrels are turned into table stands. It gives it a rustic, piratey touch. Hellooooo sailor! Reminds me of Guy Fawkes and gunpowder plots. Fuck me.... barely five sips into this al fresco Balantine and I am losing my sight. The end is nigh. Call my trumpeters and emissaries. This is it. I am done for. Tonight I must surely die. Yes, 'tis tonight, right here, my last and very darkest moment in Spain. My god. Or do I mean *Dios mío!* Excuse, now, my spelling and expletives or random moments of coming ineligibility, but it has all been quite beyond words to express, and beyond my wildest dreams. This trip. Good lord. How will I ever adjust back to my old ways after this? No contact with home for days, not since I left for Conil. Should have done so really, but I am alive and will probably return in one piece. Girlfriend sounded a bit rum on last email contact.

"Spiritual awakenings." I wrote.

"Spiritually dead." was the response.

Yikes. I could have asked what she was on about, but the truth is, I didn't want to know. The less in my brain the better at times like these, when I am just free-falling into the blue. Damned, but not forgotten. Waiting now for someone, anyone, to ask for a song or just keep me company. I am lonely somehow, but aren't we all? Playing stops me smoking, that is something good at least. I am drowning in ridiculous

The Road to El Palmar

amounts of whisky right now, and the words I write get smaller and have become more like straight lines. Fuck me, I am pissed beyond all recognition. Help. S.O.S. A n y o n e ? Each letter coming out now, one by one and quite a task to achieve. This is it folks. The boat is going down. Writing is a skill that I barely remember learning, but right now am kumquat grapefruit for. I wonder how many ladies go home dreaming of me tonight. The dashing troubadour who came to play Jerez. Life sucks ever such a bit sometimes. Though some kids took my photo. Woohoo! Shades were down at the time, so I was happy to oblige, but noticed a sneaky dude doing some long distance camera work some way behind them.

'No Chromatica!' Was what the man in Prague shouted at me. I was on the bridge trying to take his photo. He was really quite insistent and then started to chase me up the road when I ignored him. Fair play.

The inconsequential looking girl, the one over there, that I mentioned when they first came in, or maybe I did not. Either way. She is kind of bland looking, and yet alive with life at the same time. Doesn't hide from me now like she did earlier, she is listening to her friend as she gabs on. Nearly got a smile. I can tell she is long bored of listening to her friend. The bar is soon to be closing. I am lonesome. Somehow I manage to finish the Bizantine behemoth, and for some stupid reason I order another. The girl behind the bar laughing, the man-waiter-beast looking incredibly unhappy, fussing about my table like a flappy twat, zoom zooming like a bi-plane. Yes I mean that. I may indulge myself to be the last man standing in this bar, thank you very much. If you want a fight about that, then I will take you all on, her too. Though on second thoughts, I might take that back as I cant seem to get off this chair at all. I know being drunk is pretty ugly, but you know what, so what.

[I scratched something out here that was probably quite puerile and sexually degenerate.] Did I really just write that? Well it flies in the face of all that is right, and holy, and correct I suppose. But isn't that the whole point? Do the deeds, and learn what pleasure there is in being so wrong that you are a god damn heretic to all. Believe me when I tell you that your heroes have dreamed of nothing less than... Oh man. Alcohol goes

City of wild Spanish horses

nowhere good. But then again, it's just human nature, and the sooner you get with it, the sooner you can progress to more elevated climes, and chimes, and songs, and sing-alongs. Songs, romance, a world where love is all that matters in the end. I went down. I fell. And hit the goddamn bottom, and broke my soul down there. I survived to write this day to say. Maybe I am a gentleman, a lover, a sinner, a grinner, and a winner. And of course, a drunk. Right now at least. And yes, I play my music in the sun. And maybe one unexpected night the hounds of hell will come looking for you in your sleep and whisper sweet ecstasy in your ear, just moments before they tear your life apart. And my enemies. I have a few. Where did they all begin, or get off? The evil in men's souls. What is that? When do we find out that the value of true living is found in love and sacrifice, and taking our time to enjoy life. Not seeing the parasites perish in vengeance. Oh lord. Vengeance. That I wanted for so long. I need healing. Forgiveness. I know this. When true love returns like a devastating light of holy goodness. Fuck…. I had my chance, and like I knew I would, I blew it. Oh man. I have a feeling that...

My last few words in the book of destiny remained incomplete, I left the bar so drunk that I forgot to pay. I knew this would happen sooner or later. In UK you buy, then you pay. In Spain you buy, and when you have finally done all you can do, *then* you pay. The flappy bi-plane waiter man chased me down the street. He seemed extraordinarily okay about it all, considering I had been giving him a bit of a hard time all night. Of course I paid, and then threw in a five euro tip by way of compensation, the bicuspid whisky obviously partly responsible for my ridiculous generosity, though really it was partly their fault.

"Sorry about Trafalgar." I said to him, as he took the money.

I eventually found, and then entered, room seven of Hostel Saliva. I stripped and lay on the bed. I wondered how I would get to morning without any drinking water, I was bone dry, and that was the last thought I had.

The pilgrim's end

When I wake at 8 am, it is to discover that my room has no windows. I had not noticed this before. It's pitch black in here, though I know it must be daylight outside from the time on my watch. I dreamed last night, firstly, of a giant black cockroach foaming on its back, then of a place that looked like Northolt church but it was getting knocked down, and then in my last dream I was at a festival organising some buskers with violins and guitars for a rendition of *"What shall we do with the drunken sailor"*. I left the festival field and entered a room to find a woman I know in there. I started to kiss her passionately, and then left back out to the buskers, who by this time had got themselves together, but were playing a completely different song, and it was then that I woke up.

I have not seen that woman in many years, and have no idea why she has appeared in a dream. I did not even know her all that well, but her brother was a very close friend for a long time, though we have long since lost touch. I lie in bed thinking about this curious aspect of what was already some pretty bizarre dreaming. I am very hungover, and deservedly so. I hurt quite a lot, in fact. It is time for that well-earned bath. I am annoyed at myself about last night, more because the drinks cost me seven euros each, and then I stupidly gave that five euro tip on top. I should have done a bloody runner and let him chase me. Oh well, it's what holidays are all about, throwing wasteful money at pointless things. And judging from what I wrote in my notes, I was in quite a state by the end of the night.

So it's my last day. I am extremely thirsty, and I forgot to buy water before coming back here last night. I don't think I get breakfast in this place either. I shall get bathed and washed, and will head out to eat somewhere. I won't move about too much today with the damn rucksack in tow. Then I'll head to the airport at about 6 pm, catch a cab to be in time for a 9:45 pm flight. Early but better to be safe, I am a stickler for getting to airports with many hours to go before a flight,

The pilgrim's end

that way I never have to run in panic. Hope there aren't any delays either. If there are not, then I will hit Blighty at 11:30 pm tonight and should be home an hour later.

I wonder what my last day holds in store. No idea what the weather is like yet, as I lie here trying to get inspired to get up. Last time I was in a room with no windows was a miserable experience, it was in Edinburgh, many years ago, and just after leaving my first girlfriend, I was in a terrible mess.

Will this dream of a trip fade into obscurity when I get home? Right now I don't know? I am sure that some of the best moments in all of our lives are lost to hazy memories, buried somewhere in our minds and later conjured in sleep. This journey was a special one, definitely some kind of pilgrimage for me. I am not sure what I was expecting, but I realise that I was driven to come, and only in coming have I had the perspective and solitude to be able to start to ask - *why did I come out here exactly?* I feel like changes are occurring in my life at a deeper level than I can grasp at the moment. Something to do with my age, maybe, something to do with the way we evolve from one kind of person into another, and maybe how we fail to do that too. I have a hunch the next few years may be quite challenging. I hope I have gained some insight from this trip, into what I need to do next for myself. It has been a tough year since becoming 37 years old, and I am not sure the worst of it has even arrived yet. The last couple of years, in fact, it has become apparent that what once had meaning and value for me, no longer seems to. I am caught on rails and need to find a new direction in life, and I think this trip was about the start of me considering that.

As I left the Hostel to find breakfast, an English couple that had sat next to me in the bar last night were there. We had a quick chin-wag. I think he was a bit of a volleyball fanatic, they had been down near Tarifa at Canos de Bayos, I think he called it. They said it was great. They offered me a lift to the airport, but its too early for me yet, which is a shame. Would have saved me lots of hassle and legwork. My craving for tomatoes and oil at an all time high. I generally avoid tomatoes in UK, yet out here I crave them.

The Road to El Palmar

What does it mean to dream of upside-down giant black cockroaches foaming from their belly? The thought is more disgusting now I am awake than it was in my dream. Like a scene from *Naked Lunch*, the film by William Burroughs. How do we decipher dreams, assuming they should be deciphered at all? Jung thought they held clues to follow that help keep the mind, body, and soul in balance, even restore it. I think he was right to some extent. Dreams are rarely direct, but more often steeped in symbolism. I also find they rarely give their wisdom up without a lot of thinking about. Having said that, it could just be the brain taking a dump. Though I feel disgusted even to think about the dream cockroach, I guess it's a good sign that it is dead. I wonder about it some more, but nothing much reveals itself. Then I wonder about the woman in my dream, and wonder what she was doing in my head after all these years, still nothing further reveals on that either. I don't feel fully functional yet. I have now had breakfast, but it's gonna be a good couple of hours before I am back on track. I need some meditation time.

So, I sit in the market place, on the steps of the obelisk feature that stands there, and do a bit of reflexology on my feet - a trick I picked up from my step mum who does it professionally - it works wonders on hangovers and colds too.

They sell snails by the bucket load in Jerez, the sellers set up in the street to catch the passers-by. They look like the same sort of snails that crawled all over my tent. Worth remembering if you ever got stuck out there and were hungry enough. These snails are everywhere in the country. Don't fancy the thought myself.

A few tourists are milling about dressed in bright colours with maps and babies. I never really was one for getting into the architecture and culture. I like action and mayhem, a bit of adventure, you can keep your pretty castles and museums and your guided tours. Unless they have something relevant to the spirit of man, then maybe. Went once with my family to an old prison, up high in the hills in Corsica. Disused now, but a long history of murderous torture and executions had occurred there. They all loved it, and got right into the history of the whole thing. I felt sick for a day after, and I swear that I had to fight for my life against possession by dark spirits the next

The pilgrim's end

night. I think something tried to follow me home. The place reeked of death and quite freaked me out from the moment we arrived. As soon as I walked in, I knew it was trouble, and I took the first chance to make a dash for the exit. I remember seeing my families faces as they poked their heads into dark rooms of stone and said *ooh* and *aah* and *really, they did that to them in here did they?* I could not understand why everyone was feeling okay, I was far from it.

I try to avoid places like that now, when you are a teenager no one gives you the choice, they think you are just being difficult. The same thing happened to me at Alhambra. I went with the girlfriend and a couple of our friends, we were driving around southern Spain last year and it was one of our stops. We stayed the night there in a hostel. I couldn't sleep. Something kept touching me each time I dropped into slumber and it woke me up. Kept happening. Never had direct physical experience of it quite like that before, never that intense. Usually it is just stuff out of the corner of my eye that makes me jump suddenly but when I look, nothing is there. That night in Alhambra it was relentless. Things flying about the room, not physically but wisps and lights that I could not quite focus on to be sure. I tried to convince myself that I was just tired and that it was my imagination. Maybe it was. I hardly slept a wink. We all got up the next day to visit the ruins there, I was too knackered to be interested. Stewart, the other guy who was with us, then said he had been kept awake all night by ghosts. I couldn't believe it. I was not the only one. The girls? They had slept like babies, of course. We generally assume it is women that are sensitive to these things and not men, but I think men just avoid talking about it. I don't know what it is, or even if it is real or just imaginary, but it is something, and it ruins my sleep when it shows up in a place.

Now, why am I writing this stuff while sat here in Jerez market place I wonder. I guess I am thinking about this stuff because of that damn weird cockroach dream, it had a similar flavour. Something succubus. Energy drainage. Insects out to get us. *Starship Troopers*, there is another film ahead of it's time and hitting a curious spot. *Aye-aye-aye*. I need to clear my mind and get a bit more positive about the day.

The Road to El Palmar

I look about the market place. Busy already at 10:30 am, I guess it's a city after all. I'll relax a while and see what gives. As much as there is beauty here, there is also a plethora of plump and scary looking old women too, theres a lot of them in south-west Spain in fact. So updating my thoughts on yesterday, it's one good reason for considering things quite carefully before marrying a Spanish girl. Someone once told me a good piece of advice, to check the mother of a woman you planned to date, because that would be 80 percent of what your chosen lady would eventually become like herself. Italians, I have noticed, seem to evolve into some kind of mammoth troll not long after marriage and breeding. Is this a terrible observation to make? The Spanish seem to have a similar trend. They can be a hard and crooked looking bunch, but despite my fickle judgements, I actually like them a lot.

'CALL A COLL OH COLKOMADEY!' Hollers the snail seller.

He has such a funny way in his sales pitch. I have been watching him for a while now. As soon as his shout begins, his hands come up to his chest and his fingers flex forward in time with his shout, then they curl around as his whole body goes into his pitch. His eyes stare down at his beloved snails as he unleashes his call, it is as if he is in a trance all the while. Then, just as the shout ends, his hands go either behind his back, or to his nuts. He looks around then, with a cheeky grin, to see who is ready to buy some snails. No one yet, not since I have been here, but he seems very happy. He has his thing.

I've been in the square enjoying the world going by. It's now noon, and I still can't shake the hangover properly. Been practising internal silence, but it's especially hard in crowds, so much going on that is distracting. The worst distraction, for me, being tits and ass. I really find that old instinct is very tough to switch off. The wolf jumping out each time something goes by. Now trying to look in glances in order to stop my laser-beams locking onto targets. Damn hard, though. Life is so rich, and full of infinitely deep rabbit-holes, we have to find a way to accept that there really isn't enough time to fit in them all. We must be choosy. I decide that will do for this mornings entertainment, and then change location to a bar. Peeing relieves me of some toxins from last night, and I start to feel a bit more human again. Maybe breakfast

The pilgrim's end

is finally starting to work.

Well, that was a somewhat gross experience. The peculiar gentleman in the pharmacy, with hair like a slick, black, boot-brush, just stroked my hand when he gave me change for my sun-block lip salve. I check that he hasn't given me lipstick. He stares at me now through the window, as I sit on the bench opposite. Damned if I am moving just because he is there. Where is a woman when you need one? Don't look his way again, he'll only misread it. I never much care if anyone is gay, but I do object to being fondled. I mean, it doesn't bother me if you want to stick it up a guy because I know which team I bat for, and neither do I fear that some latent homosexual tendency is likely to come bursting out of me at this stage of my life. I spent a lot of time at Trade in Turnmills, a night club in London that was popular in the '90s. You were supposed to be gay to get in, but the doorman back then was cool about it. Best club I ever went to. It was wild and tribal on the edge of rational horizons. A lot of friends came out of the closet down there, some of them dragged out probably a bit unfairly not so much because they were gay, but because they took too many ecstasy pills and someone-else decided to try to persuade them that they were. I knew the deal from the start, having been at an all-boys boarding school for five years it teaches you about handling such things. Sure, I dabbled and played when younger, it's just pleasure receptors being triggered after all.

Jesus! He is still stood motionless over there like Hannibal Lecter, his staring eyes burning holes into me from a distance. Creepy. What a strange end to a curious trip. I sigh, and blow out some smoke, leaning back into the bench. Feels like it has been a long day, a long week, a long life. I check the time. Yup, I really ought to be thinking about heading off. I don't know if I am looking forward to my return to England or not. I don't know much right now, and I guess that doesn't matter much either. It's been interesting. An incredible trip. The first I have written up and reported on in such a way, and that has been quite good fun too. I have no idea what comes next in my life, but I have a feeling that this journey may have had an impact. It felt right to come. It did feel like some kind of pilgrimage once it got started, but now it is time to face the music and roll the credits.

I pick up my guitar, fling my over-weight rucksack up on my shoulders, and I start to make my way towards the airport and to home.

Other books by Mark DK Berry

Non-fiction

The Experience, A Gentleman's Guide to Threesomes: Exploring Relationship, Sexual Energy & Western Tantra

Fiction

Pussy Productions

Poetry (Also available as Audiobooks)

Broke: Poetry & Lyrics: Poetry Collection, Book 1
Leaving Town: Chasing Dreams that Run Away Like Cats Down Alleys After Midnight

The above titles are available via Amazon -
https://www.amazon.com/author/markberry

To find out more about all other publications visit www.mdkberry.com

Music by Mark DK Berry

Mark DK Berry is also a published musician, producer, and songwriter. Works published through international record labels, as well as all other productions, are available through the web site www.mdkberry.com

www.ingramcontent.com/pod-product-compliance
Lightning Source LLC
LaVergne TN
LVHW090116080426
835507LV00040B/908